WOW! MOMENTS

"I must start with 'WOW!' This beautiful, soulful, and wonder-filled book is written with such down to earth candor, humor, and authenticity. I laughed and cried out loud in recognition of the beauty and holy design of life so synergistically depicted for the readers. What a beautiful and uplifting tool for life."

Jayne Atkinson, Tony Award nominee for the Broadway shows, *The Rainmaker* and *Enchanted April*

"For years I attended Rev. Billy Hester's church in Savannah, Georgia. When I moved back to New York City, I continued listening to his sermons on the Asbury Memorial website and found myself frequently sharing them with friends and colleagues in both my Christian and Jewish communities. I am so pleased that I can now give them this book of 'Wow moments' which exemplifies Reverend Billy's ministry, passion, faith, and wisdom!"

Rev. Eleanor Harrison Bregman, Director of Multi-Faith Initiatives, Romemu Synagogue, New York City

"As someone who has experienced first-hand the immense pain of losing too many loved ones, of a career which has caused me to experience more ups and downs than I care to count, I will admit to asking these questions: 'Is God really there? Is He watching with care, and is He truly on my side?' Billy Hester's book is an encouragement for all to take a hard look back at their lives and see the wonder of God's work within them. They may undoubtedly find such moments and feel relief that He truly is there. That if one keeps one's eyes, ears, and heart open, they will experience the wonder of His work behind the scenes and may be able to carry on with gratitude and a genuine light heart, eventually learning and living with confidence to let go, let God, and say, 'WOW!'"

Robert Cuccioli, Tony Award nominee for the Broadway musical, *Jekyll and Hyde*

"This little volume contains remarkable stories drawn from the intersection of Billy Hester's long and creative career as both a New York performer and a local parish minister. Some of them will strike you as pleasantly coincidental while others are nothing less than chilling and miraculous. If you are facing one of life's challenges or tempted to think that you are alone in the universe, read this book."

Rev. Dr. John M. Finley, Senior Minister, First Baptist Church, Savannah, Georgia

"In a world filled with personal apprehension, anxiety, and even tragedy, we are privileged to have people like Billy Hester in our lives. He helps us recognize the Wow moments we've all experienced. It is these instances, where all the stars align in our lives, when the fates turn in our favor, that we understand the wondrous nature of the world. We are so blessed in so many ways, and it is people like Billy Hester who help us focus our attention on all of these blessings."

Rabbi Robert Haas, Congregation Mickve Israel, Savannah, Georgia

"In sharing the joyful stories of 'grace, wonder, and synchronicity' from his life, Rev. Billy has written a book which both entertains and surprises. More importantly though, through his lifelong practice of paying attention, he gently teaches us to capture the fleeting 'wow!' moments in our own lives, so that they might spark a little more daily faith and wake us up in times when God feels too much absent. This collection is filled with the same generosity and grace that animates Billy's ministry and is a great addition to the spiritual bookshelf!"

Rev. David H. Messner, Minister, Unitarian Universalist Church, Savannah, Georgia

WOW! MOMENTS

Stories of Grace, Wonder, and Synchronicity

Billy Hester

Billy Hester Books, LLC / Savannah, Georgia

WOW! Moments
Stories of Grace, Wonder, and Synchronicity
by Billy Hester

Published by Billy Hester Books, LLC, Savannah, Georgia, USA
Printed by CreateSpace, An Amazon.com Company
Available from Amazon.com and other retail outlets

ISBN 978-0-9979-9810-8

To my mother,
Joan Hester Byrd,
the "songbird" of Asbury,
and to her singing partner
and my number one advisor,
Phillip H. Hunter, Sr.,
who made his transition just
before this book was published,
and to the fellow who taught me
to play hard and dream big,
Butch Hester.

Contents

ACKNOWLEDGMENTS

I would like to acknowledge the enormous help given to me in creating this book. Thanks for the cheerleaders and proofreaders: Pat Andres, Wayne Bland, Susan Bolinger, Iris Dayoub, Barry Parker, Kate Strain, and my wife, Cheri.

Thanks also to the parishioners of the churches I've had the privilege of serving—Marble Collegiate Church in New York City and Wesley Monumental United Methodist Church, Wesley Oak United Methodist Church, and Asbury Memorial United Methodist Church in Savannah, Georgia. I especially want to thank the members of Asbury Memorial for giving me the encouragement to write this book and the time off in the summer to complete it.

A special thank you goes to Claudette DeLong, Randy Canady, and Ray Ellis—members of our church staff who worked extra hard during the summer while I was away writing.

Last, but not least, I want to thank Frank Ramsey, an Asbury member who helped me edit, design, and publish this book. Thanks, Frank—I couldn't have done it without you!

Introduction: Not-So-Everyday Miracles

"Where are you, Lord? I need you. Please give me a sign! Let me know that you are real and that you care."

Many people have similar thoughts at some time in their life. These feelings can occur when we lose a close relationship or when we've been downsized out of a job or when we've been given sobering news from a physician. As we all know, it's not too difficult to feel good about our faith when things are going well. It's when tragedy strikes or something doesn't go our way that God often feels absent and our faith is shaken.

The writers of the Hebrew Scriptures experienced these same feelings. In the psalms of lament, a person cries out, "How long, O Lord? Will you forget me forever? How long will you hide your face from me? How long must I bear pain in my soul, and have sorrow in my heart all day long?" (Psalm 13:1-2a).

These are normal feelings that even Jesus of Nazareth expressed. As a Jew in first-century Israel, Jesus grew up learning the Hebrew Scriptures. He was very familiar with the laments in the Book of Psalms. When he was dying on the cross, he echoed the feelings of the psalmist who wrote: "My God, my God, why have you forsaken me?" (Psalm 22:1a).

When we are suffering, we want to know where God is. We want to know if God cares and if God can help us. Like Tevye in *Fiddler on the Roof* conversing with the Almighty, we feel like saying, "Lord, it would be nice, if on occasion, you would give me a sign on a silver platter—or at least on a paper plate!"

It appears that's not how God works. God is not a magician who gives us signs and wonders whenever we desire. That's a genie, and there are not too many of those around.

So in times of despair, how do we keep our faith? How do we keep going when we feel alone and abandoned?

Fortunately, we have tools to help sustain us through difficult periods in our life. Among these important resources are prayer, scripture, liturgy, music, worship, exercise, faith communities, and our family and friends. Where would we be without these important life preservers? They've offered us strength and comfort many times over.

As great as these resources are, wouldn't it be wonderful if once in a while something miraculous happened that revealed to us that God is real and active in our lives? Wouldn't it be wonderful if something happened that was so profound and spectacular that it affirmed our belief in a caring and present deity?

Of course, God does do spectacular things for us every day—with the rising of the sun, the beauty of nature, and a host of other miraculous things we often take for granted. As

I write these words, I'm sitting in the mountains of North Carolina where it's easy to feel the bigness and awesomeness of God as I gaze across the Smokies. When I'm home in Savannah, Georgia, and go to the beach on Tybee Island, it's easy to sense God's presence as I run my toes through the sand and gaze out at an endless ocean. We have these feelings when we witness the birth of a child and when we see a person forgive someone who has harmed them. There are countless miracles that reveal the wonder and presence of God. These miracles could be considered natural miracles that we experience every day—miracles we have come to expect.

This book wants to consider the *not-so-everyday* miracles—things that make us go, "Wow! That's incredible!" Yes, a jaw-dropping sunset or a huge super-moon can make us go, "Wow!" But I am referring to things that seem out of the ordinary—things that psychiatrist Carl Jung called moments of *synchronicity*.

Jung defined synchronicity as "an acausal connection of two or more psycho-physic phenomena." For those of us who prefer less scientific language, synchronicity is when two or more circumstances come together in a coincidental and meaningful way. These unique coincidences often inspire people to think more deeply about their lives and their faith. So these moments are not simply coincidences, they are *meaningful* coincidences.

No one is more surprised about me writing a book on this topic than I am. There was a time when I believed that God had given us the gift of life and the gift of free choice and then said, "Now, have at it, folks. Let's see what you can do." I cringe when I hear people say, "It was God's will," or some other trite phrase that shirks human responsibility. God isn't a puppeteer controlling us. God desires us to make good choices and to be co-creators of God's kingdom on earth.

But I have come to realize that my theology was just as limited and dualistic as the theology of those who put everything into God's basket. I was doing the same thing: assuming to know what God could and could not do. Instead of God doing everything, I believed God wasn't doing much of anything. That's not quite true. I actually believed God was doing a lot. But it was all from the inside out. I believed that through God's Spirit, God gave us the strength, the patience, the courage, the peace—whatever it is we needed—to live meaningful, purposeful lives. For me, God's activity was always something that went through us, not beyond us.

Today I'm in a different place. I still believe that God gives us free will. I still believe that God works in and through us—that God desires human beings to make choices that further peace, justice, and love. But I also believe that God is active in ways we do not understand and in ways we can't anticipate. Jesus said that when people are touched by God's Spirit, the experience is filled with mystery: "The wind blows where it chooses, and you hear the sound of it, but you do not know where it comes from or where it goes" (John 3:8). This mysterious dimension of the movement of God's Spirit has taken me to a place where I now believe that God works in us, through us, and *beyond* us.

Why this change?

One of the things that prompted this new appreciation for the mysterious work of the Spirit was my discovery of

Christian mystics. I learned more about ancient mystics like Teresa of Avilla and Meister Eckhart, along with more contemporary mystics such as Evelyn Underhill and Matthew Fox. These voices, along with theologians Richard Rohr, Leslie Weatherhead, and Marcus Borg, inspired me to discover more about contemplative prayer, *Lectio Divina*, and other Christian practices that celebrate the Spirit and mystery.

For example, in his book, *On Learned Ignorance*, the 15th century German theologian and astronomer, Nicholas of Cusa, said that there are at least three kinds of ignorance that show up in those who seek God. First, there are those who do not know that they do not know. Then, there are those who know that they do not know but who think they ought to know. Finally, there are those who know that they do not know and who receive this learned ignorance as God's own gift—because it relieves them from the terrible burden of thinking they have to know everything God knows. It frees them to live in a state of perpetual wonder. Nicholas says that this is very high-level ignorance.

I also became intrigued with the growing relationship between science and religion. By religion, I don't mean the institutional church with its dogmas and creeds; I mean the belief in a Higher Power and the reality of a Spirit, Life Force, Energy, Zoe, or whatever one wants to call this Positive Force that brings life. This Spirit or Energy is a key part of both science and religion. In fact, it is getting more and more difficult to see where science ends and religion begins—and vice versa. Even most skeptics believe our earthly life is not all there is. We know there's another level of reality, another dimension, a spiritual dimension. The French theologian and scientist, Teilhard de Chardin, said it clearly: "We are not human beings seeking a spiritual experience. We are spiritual beings having a human experience."

But the main reason for my change in perspective has been my *experiences*. Like the apostle Thomas, there was part of me that wouldn't believe in supernatural coincidences unless I could see and experience them myself. Well, I have. I've experienced profound moments of grace, wonder, and synchronicity many times over. My suspicion is that you have too.

There's a possibility that I wouldn't have developed an appreciation for these divine coincidences had I not begun writing them down. For you see, I had difficulty remembering them. Something remarkable would happen in my life, and I would reflect on it for a while. But eventually the meaningful coincidence would fade away and dissolve from my memories. It was as if the incredible experience never happened.

I discovered this tendency when I decided to record a wow experience in a journal. I simply wrote down what had happened. Several years later I was going through a rough patch in my life when God seemed absent. While going through my files, I came across the paper on which I had recorded the wow moment a few years earlier. I couldn't believe it. I had forgotten all about it. As I read what I had written, I realized how much I had felt loved and supported by God at the time. When I remembered the event, I felt better and more at peace. I was reminded of God's presence and power.

Realizing that I had forgotten all about this wow moment, I wondered how many other wow moments I had failed to remember. I decided that if I had any more meaningful coincidences, I would write them down. I didn't expect to have many. I didn't want to consider just any old coincidence. It had to be something unbelievable—something that made me go, "Wow! That's incredible!" I assumed that I would be fortunate to have two or three such experiences in my lifetime. To my surprise, I've had many more. Twenty-five of them are recorded in this book. God had been at work and active in my life much more than I had realized.

I have learned the importance of writing such experiences down, and I encourage you to do the same. Create a "WOW! Journal," a notebook filled with the moments of grace, wonder, and synchronicity that you experience. I suspect that what happened to me will happen to you—you'll discover that you've had a lot more wow moments than you realize.

When life feels extra challenging and you feel as though the wind has been knocked out of your sails, go to your "WOW! Journal." Open it and read about the amazing things you have experienced. It will remind you that God is present and working in your life. It will strengthen your faith and offer you peace.

I once heard someone say, "We can *experience* God more than we can explain God." I agree. That's what happens through our wow moments *and* our "WOW! Journals." We can't explain why and how things happen—we can't explain God—but we can experience God and God's love and grace through these meaningful coincidences.

Since this book offers uplifting and amazing stories, I am

concerned that some readers may get the impression that I view life through rose-colored glasses. Let me assure you that I don't. I do believe that life is better when we are able to have faith and a positive attitude. But I also realize that life is very difficult and is often not fair.

My father died of a heart attack at the age of 35 when I was four years old. When I was 23, my stepfather drowned in a boating accident at the age of 58. As a husband, I know the challenges of marriage. As a father of four, I know the difficulties in raising children. As a minister, I have been with parishioners who have had ALS, Spinal Muscular Atrophy, AIDS, brain tumors, and various cancers. Life is tough. We only have to turn on the news or go on the Internet to see the turmoil that is all over the world. It's very easy to get discouraged.

That's one reason I'm writing this book. We need all of the resources we can get to strengthen our faith and to be comforted by God's presence. I can't tell you how many times the stories in my "WOW! Journal" have helped me during times of stress and anxiety.

The first stories in this book occurred when I lived in New York City, pursuing a career in theatre. Most of the other stories happened after I moved back to my hometown of Savannah, Georgia. Since much of my career has been in the ordained ministry and since I have been at the same church since 1993, many of the stories involve the members of Asbury Memorial United Methodist Church in Savannah. I thank everyone who is part of these stories for sharing their lives with me and for inspiring me through these wow moments.

A few of the stories in this book may not seem to have the wow factor that many of the others have—they may feel like simple coincidences. But because of the *huge* wow moments I have experienced; I have found myself considering God's involvement in things I normally would not have considered.

Thank you for taking the time to read parts of my "WOW! Journal." Hopefully these stories will encourage you and strengthen your faith. Mostly, I hope they will inspire you to create your own "WOW! Journal," so that you can be encouraged by the moments of grace, wonder, and synchronicity that have occurred in your own life.

Blessings and Peace
Billy

THE CUTE, SHORT-HAIRED BLONDE

As an ordained minister, I have had the opportunity to officiate many weddings. When meeting with a couple to plan their marriage ceremony, I often ask them how they met. Usually a knowing grin comes across the face of the bride or groom, signaling that they have a story to tell—and a story that they feel is a "good one."

I have a good one too. In fact, it is so good that it's the first thing that happened in my life that made me start thinking more seriously about synchronicity and the movement of God's Spirit beyond us.

I grew up in Savannah, Georgia, long before *Midnight in the Garden of Good and Evil* and the Savannah College of Art and Design had people flocking from all over the world to the old port city. As a youngster, I developed a great love for singing and drama. I decided to pursue a career in musical theatre and attended Valdosta State College in Valdosta, Georgia, where I received a BFA in Theatre in 1981. The next step was New York City and, hopefully, Broadway.

Through a summer-stock experience in New Jersey, I met a fellow actor who needed a roommate to split the rent of his tiny Manhattan apartment. I took him up on his offer and moved into the small space at 43 East 29th Street. As I was becoming familiar with the neighborhood, I noticed a beautiful church on the corner of 29th Street and Fifth Avenue, Marble Collegiate Church. On the marquee was the name Norman Vincent Peale. I had heard about Dr. Peale and his book, *The Power of Positive Thinking.*

Trying to make it as an actor in New York, I figured I needed as much positive thinking as I could get; so I started attending the worship services there. I learned that Marble was one of the oldest Protestant churches in America. Since the church was so close to my apartment, I could roll out of bed and into the sanctuary within ten minutes for a good dose of Dr. Peale's positivity.

One of the first persons I met at Marble was an actor named David Schall. David wanted to form a prayer and support group for actors and other people in the arts. He asked me to be part of this new group that would be called "The Actors' Fellowship." Since the Broadway shows were dark on Mondays, we planned to meet at the church every Monday at 5:30 p.m. Around 20 to 40 of us would gather each week for study, prayer, and fellowship.

After a year of meeting together, David encouraged us to reach out to more people in the entertainment industry. He designed a special event to draw more actors, singers, dancers, directors, choreographers, and other persons in the performing arts. Besides focusing on our faith, the event would also offer practical information about the business side of a theatrical career—such as auditioning, getting an agent, and preparing a picture and résumé.

The event was held in March of 1983 in Bay Hall at Marble

Collegiate. There were 60 to 80 people in attendance—including about 25 first-timers. One of the visitors caught my eye—a cute, short-haired blonde. I became mesmerized as I glanced at her from a distance. It was like that famous scene in *West Side Story* when Tony and Maria see each other for the first time across the dance floor. The only problem was that the girl did not see me. It was only Tony looking at Maria.

"Who is she?" I wondered. I assumed that someone from our leadership team had invited the actress because her picture and résumé were posted on the bulletin board as an example of what a professional headshot and résumé should look like. It was impressive. She was impressive. I wanted to meet her. But there were a few hurdles standing in the way.

For one, this girl looked way out of my league. Secondly, she already seemed to be an established actress, and I was a rookie. Thirdly, she most likely had a boyfriend. After considering these obstacles, I became intimidated and decided not to introduce myself. I didn't even find out her name.

I told myself that if she came back to The Actors' Fellowship the following week, I would be more assertive and would meet her. After all, it would be one of our regular meetings and a much smaller group—more conducive to getting to know someone. I'm not sure that was true, but it was how I rationalized it. In the end, it really didn't matter; the cute blonde did not return.

The following week, however, brought some good news. I got a call from an agent for an audition.

At the time, I did not have an agent, but I was able to borrow one from someone else. A friend named Cortlandt

Hull knew Mae Questel, the great character actress who had supplied the voices of the cartoon characters Betty Boop and Olive Oyl. Mae also was known for her hilarious portrayal of Aunt Bethany in *National Lampoon's Christmas Vacation.* Our mutual friend, Cortlandt, lived in Connecticut. He was making a trip to New York and was going to visit Mae while he was in Manhattan. He asked if I wanted to meet the legendary actress. I said, "Of course!"

Mae was gracious enough to invite us to her beautiful Manhattan apartment for lunch. When she discovered that I did not have an agent, Mae said she would ask her agent if he would send me on some auditions. Having an agent is very helpful for a performer because agents know about auditions that are not publicized. Plus, they're able to get you an appointment for the audition. "I can't promise you anything," Mae said in that distinctive voice of hers, "but I will see what I can do." It was such a thoughtful gesture, especially since she had just met me. I will never forget the kindness of Mae Questel.

A few days after the luncheon, I actually got a call from Mae's agent—Mae had come through! Jack Bateman from The Bee Beck Talent Agency said he had an audition for me. It was for the musical *Pippin,* being staged at Theatre by the Sea in Portsmouth, New Hampshire. I had played the title role of *Pippin* in a community production in Savannah, so I was very familiar with the role. I learned that the director and staff from Portsmouth had already been to New York once for auditions. They had cast all of the roles, except for the lead character of Pippin. I'm not sure why they had difficulty casting someone when they came to Manhattan the first time.

There were plenty of unemployed actors in New York who could have played the role deftly. Apparently, the director and his production team hadn't seen anyone they wanted to cast. So they came all the way back to New York to try to cast the role again. I auditioned; and, to my surprise, they offered me the role.

The show was going to be rehearsed and performed in Portsmouth. I had a car and was planning to drive to New Hampshire. Most actors in New York don't have a vehicle, so I called Jack, the agent, and asked if he thought any of the other cast members would want to ride to Portsmouth with me. He said, "Why don't you call the girl playing opposite you? I have her name and number." The girl's name was Cheri Butcher. I called her, but got her answering service. I left my name and number.

Later that day, the actress called me back and explained that she was currently out of town, performing in a show in Los Angeles. I introduced myself and told her that I was in the cast of *Pippin*. I shared that I would be driving to Portsmouth and I wondered if she wanted to ride with me. She said that would be great.

The following Monday, two weeks after seeing the cute, short-haired blonde at Marble Collegiate, I attended another Actors' Fellowship meeting. The cute, short-haired blonde still was not there. I needed to let it go and move on. Besides, I had much to be thankful for. The majority of actors were out of work, and here I was, just cast in the lead role of a musical.

We circled in a small group and took turns sharing what the week had brought us. Some people talked about their past auditions, others shared about upcoming auditions, while others focused on more practical goals—like getting new résumés, getting headshots, or finding an agent. When it came my turn to speak, I said that I had some good news—I had been cast as Pippin in a production at Theatre by the Sea in New Hampshire. Everyone cheered! I thanked them for their prayers and support. How blessed I was to have this wonderful group of friends.

After the meeting, an actress named Jodi Marzorati introduced herself to me. She was new to the group. By the way, Jodi would eventually marry a man named Ray Benson and become Jodi Benson, who would later be cast as the voice of Ariel in Disney's blockbuster film, *The Little Mermaid*.

Jodi said to me, "Congratulations on getting cast as Pippin! A close friend of mine was just cast in the same show! I think she may be playing opposite you."

"Really?" I said. "I must have just spoken to her on the phone. Is she in L.A. doing a show?"

"Yes, that's her…Cheri Butcher."

Then Jodi said something that really got my attention. "She was with me at The Actors' Fellowship a couple of weeks ago. It was her first time here too."

Then I had an unbelievable thought: Could the girl Jodi was talking about be the same girl I wanted to meet? Could the girl I wanted to meet two weeks ago be the girl I talked to in California? Could the girl I wanted to meet be riding with me all the way to New Hampshire? Could the girl I wanted to meet be playing opposite me in *Pippin*? Impossible!

The day came for the big trip to New Hampshire. On

Monday, April 11, 1983, I drove to 330 West 56th Street to pick up Cheri Butcher. Still wondering if the girl I was about to meet could possibly be the cute, short-haired blonde, I went inside the apartment building and got on the elevator. It took me to the fourth floor. I then found apartment 4E and knocked on the door. When the door opened, standing in front of me was the cute, short-haired blonde. I then heard Rod Serling say, "You have entered the Twilight Zone!"

Cheri Butcher and I had a great drive to Portsmouth. It was soon obvious to the cast that the characters of Pippin and Catherine were not only an item on stage, but behind it as well. After the production of *Pippin* was over, we went back to Manhattan and dated for four years. On June 27, 1987, we married at Marble Collegiate Church, the place where I first saw Cheri.

Cheri and I have been blessed. There have been peaks and valleys in our relationship as there are in every relationship. But we are blessed to have each other and blessed to have four amazing children.

Cheri often reminds me that there is one part of this remarkable story that I often leave out when I share it with people. When I met Cheri, I was dating another person—or at least I was trying to date her. A year before I met Cheri, I met a wonderful woman for whom I fell head over heels. She was pretty, kind, and talented. There was just one problem: she was a great deal older than me. Although the age difference didn't concern me, it concerned her. As much as we tried to date, the age difference always seemed to get in the way. The handwriting was on the wall.

We all know how difficult it is when a relationship

doesn't work out, especially after we've invested time, energy, and our hearts. The loss of that relationship was painful for me. But it was greatly soothed by the incredible, remarkable, mystical way I met Cheri.

I am still in awe and wonder about how it all happened. I still can't get over the fact that the girl I called in California was the girl I wanted to meet in New York two weeks earlier. Every time I think about it—even after 33 years—I get goose bumps. It is simply mindboggling.

Do you know that I never got another job from all the other auditions that Jack Bateman, the agent, sent me on? When you consider the small percentage of Equity actors who are working (not to mention the non-Equity actors), when you consider that Cheri and I were cast in the same show, when you consider that I wouldn't have had the opportunity to audition for the show had it not been for Betty Boop's help, when you consider that the show's director had already been to New York to cast the role but couldn't find anyone, when you consider that I had seen Cheri just two weeks before at church, when you consider that both of us wanted something more to develop from the relationship, and finally, when you consider that Cheri is still way out of my league, it is absolutely amazing!

All I know to say is, "Thanks be to God!"

FREDERIC

Prequels seem to be popular these days. *Star Wars, Star Trek, The Wizard of Oz, Peter Pan,* and *The Planet of the Apes* all have had prequels in recent years. This next story is the prequel to my getting cast as Pippin and to meeting my wife, Cheri.

When I moved to the "Big Apple" in 1981, I knew very few people in New York—I certainly didn't have any theatrical connections. I also was not a member of the Actors' Equity Association (AEA), the union for professional actors.

If you hope to have a career as an actor, it's important to be a member of Equity, so that you can be in shows that offer union wages. Broadway shows, for instance, use Equity performers. Also, as a member of Equity, you're allowed to audition for shows that non-Equity performers do not have the opportunity to audition for. And finally, as a member of Equity, you have a better chance of getting an agent to represent you. An agent can open many doors for a performer. So it's really beneficial to have your Equity Card.

But there's a Catch-22. To receive your Equity Card, you need to be in an Equity show. *But,* in order to audition for an Equity show, you need to be a member of Equity.

Yes, it's dizzying, I know. So how can someone become a member of Equity?

Sometimes casting directors for a professional show will be open to auditioning a handful of non-Equity actors *after* they have seen all of the Equity performers, although there is no guarantee they will do this. A non-Equity performer can wait around all day at an audition and not be seen. Sometimes the people casting the show do a "cattle call" and have a huge group of actors parade in front of them, only to select a handful of them to audition. In this case, being selected to audition doesn't have anything to do with talent; rather, it's what you look like and what they are looking for in appearance.

I had been to a "zillion" Equity auditions, hoping to get into an Equity show. More times than not, I didn't even get a chance to audition. I did get cast in an Off-Broadway company called Light Opera of Manhattan (LOOM), but I did not receive a salary. Equity performers were cast in the lead roles at LOOM and were paid. Those of us who were cast in the chorus were not Equity and were not paid. We performed at LOOM for the experience and to pad our résumés.

LOOM was a repertory company that produced light operas, especially Gilbert and Sullivan operettas. We cranked them out, one right after the other: *The Mikado, The Pirates of Penzance, H.M.S. Pinafore, Ruddigor*e—if Gilbert and Sullivan wrote it, we did it. We also performed Romberg's *The Desert Song* and Victor Herbert's *The Red Mill*. It was great experience. But you can't pay rent with experience. After a year of performing at LOOM and not getting cast in any Equity shows, I decided that I needed to evaluate my career choice. I needed to go back to Savannah to ponder my future.

Just before I left New York, I learned about an audition for a production of *The Pirates of Penzance.* It was going to be at a reputable Equity regional theatre called Darien Dinner Theatre. Since I had performed in *The Pirates of Penzance* at LOOM, I was very familiar with the music of the show and was eager to audition. Perhaps having *Pirates* on my résumé would help my chances of getting cast. But would I even be seen, since I was not an Equity performer? This would be my last opportunity before leaving New York.

At the end of the auditions for the Equity performers, those of us who were non-Equity were thrilled to learn that the casting directors were willing to see some of us. I would actually get to sing! They were casting the chorus—the men who would play the ensemble of pirates. It was a paying job. If a non-Equity person was cast, he would not be getting an Equity Card; but he at least would be getting points toward his Equity Card.

After singing, the production staff asked me to stay and sing again. So I did, and they called me back again. About 14 of us remained for the 8 roles that made up the chorus of pirates. We sang again, and I made the next cut that trimmed us down to 10. This was it—I was finally going to get my big break. Then, on the last and final audition, I was cut. I couldn't believe it—Savannah, here I come.

It just so happened that during this same time, I was apartment sitting for a friend named Peter Sham. Peter and I had worked together in the chorus at LOOM and had become good friends. He was going out of town, so he asked me to watch his apartment for him while he was away. When I went over to Peter's place and took in his mail, I noticed that he received a newspaper that announced auditions for theatrical productions.

In the 1980s, there were two popular newspapers in New York that advertised auditions. I had heard that one paper was more reliable than the other, so I always purchased the one that had the better reputation. The one Peter got in the mail was the one that was supposed to be less reliable. I had never read this paper, so I decided to skim through it to see what it was like.

To my surprise, I saw an audition for another professional production of *The Pirates of Penzance*. This production of *Pirates* was going to be at a reputable regional theatre called Coachlight Dinner Theatre in Hartford, Connecticut. I did not understand. This audition was not announced in the paper that I purchased. Why wasn't this audition in the newspaper that most actors received—the paper that's supposed to be more reliable? If I hadn't been to Peter's apartment and taken in his mail, I would have never known about it. So even though I had my plane ticket to Savannah, it looked like I was going to one more audition.

When I woke up on the morning of the audition, I had an upset stomach. I didn't think I would be able to leave the apartment. But since I knew this would be my final audition and since it was a show I was familiar with, I talked myself into going. What did I have to lose anyway? I wasn't even sure if they would see me since I wasn't Equity. Out the door and onto a subway I went—arriving at the site of the audition. After all of the Equity performers were seen, the casting director and production team were willing to see about eight of us non-Equity folks who had been waiting.

After I sang for them, they asked me to sing some more—and some more—and some more. They then asked me some questions, and I went home. The next day, I got a call from the casting director, a man named Jeffrey Zeiner. He said, "Billy, how would you like to play the lead role of Frederic in *The Pirates of Penzance*?" I couldn't believe it. Was this for real?

For the director and casting agent to put their trust in me—in someone they did not know, in someone with very little New York experience, in someone who wasn't a member of Equity—was simply unbelievable. If I had gotten in the other production of *Pirates,* I only would have been in the chorus and just gotten points toward an Equity Card. But since I got the lead role in Coachlight's production of *Pirates,* I automatically received my Equity Card and became part of the union.

I had a wonderful experience at Coachlight. I got to play opposite one of the best sopranos in the business, the incomparable Connie Coit Kitchens. I became friends with theatre veterans like Paul V. Ames and Ron Owens. And I got to meet an unforgettable woman named "Ma" Yelle, who became every cast member's adopted grandmother.

It also happened to be Coachlight's 10th anniversary year. This meant that we had a special performance that included celebrity guests in the audience. One guest was the legendary actress, Joan Fontaine. Joan and her older sister, Olivia de Havilland, are the only set of siblings to have won lead acting

Oscars. What a treat it was to perform for and to meet Joan Fontaine.

This production of *The Pirates of Penzance* was also how I met Cortlandt Hull, the gentleman who introduced me to Mae Questel, the character actress who got her agent to send me on the audition for *Pippin*. So many wonderful things came out of this experience.

The popular phrase, "six degrees of separation," comes to mind when I think about what happened. This experience that transformed my life and career occurred because:

- I was in the chorus of a production of *The Pirates of Penzance* at Light Opera of Manhattan, an unpaid position, but an experience that helped me become familiar with the show and its music. This familiarity with the music helped me audition well for Coachlight's production.
- I did not get cast in the production of *The Pirates of Penzance* at Darien Dinner Theatre—the audition I thought would be my last before leaving New York. If I had gotten cast, I would not have auditioned for Coachlight's production and would not have gotten my Equity Card.
- I helped a friend by watching his apartment for him. If I had not watched Peter's apartment, I wouldn't have gotten his mail or known about the audition.
- I went to the audition, even though I felt ill and thought about not going.
- I was cast in the lead role, even though I was not a member of Equity and had little New York experience.

But this was only the beginning—because it was this experience of playing Frederic in *The Pirates of Penzance* that would lead to other circumstances and coincidences that would eventually lead me to getting cast in *Pippin* and to meeting my wife, Cheri. Without Frederic, there would have been no Pippin—and without Pippin there would have been no Cheri.

Another one of the great benefits of this wow experience happened in New York after I got back from playing Frederic in Connecticut. I got a phone call from the director of Light Opera of Manhattan—the place where I used to work for free in the chorus. The director asked me if I would be in their next production of *The Pirates of Penzance*. But this time, I would not be in the chorus. This time, I would be playing the lead role of Frederic. And this time, I would be getting paid. Needless to say, I jumped at the opportunity!

I've always found it interesting that this great career experience was made possible through something that didn't involve my career at all. It was made possible because I helped a friend. Had I not been apartment-sitting for Peter Sham, I would have never known about the audition, and I never would have been cast.

Thank you, Peter. I'll look after your place anytime!

CHRISTOPHER SEPPE AND *THE FANTASTICKS*

In 1980, I was a senior at Valdosta State College in Valdosta, Georgia, *and* a senior at Armstrong State College in Savannah, Georgia. The reason for dual colleges my senior year had a lot to do with the summer after my junior year.

During my junior year at Valdosta State, I auditioned at the Southeastern Theatre Conference in order to get a job at a summer stock theatre. I was offered a position with a theatrical company called Green Mountain Guild, a repertory company located in Vermont. So in the summer of 1980, I joined a cast of other young thespians and performed in two musicals, *Oliver* and *My Fair Lady*. We toured all over the state of Vermont—Killington, Quechee, Mt. Snow, and Stowe, home of Maria von Trapp. I have a great story about Maria, but it didn't quite meet the requirements of my "WOW! Journal." It's still a wonderful story about her thoughtfulness and generosity—perhaps it will get into a future book.

After the summer stock season was over, I drove back home to Georgia. On the way, I went through Manhattan so

I could see the long-running production of *The Fantasticks* at Sullivan Street Playhouse, a tiny Off-Broadway theatre in Greenwich Village. I fell in love with the show and its music. The character of Matt was a perfect role for me. In the New York production, a very talented actor named Christopher Seppe played the role. He was terrific as Matt. His singing voice could melt butter.

As I was preparing to go back to Valdosta State for my senior year, I learned that Armstrong State College in Savannah was producing *The Fantasticks* during the first semester. Since I was planning to move to New York after I graduated from college, I knew that I would have a better chance at getting the role of Matt in New York if I had already played the role and had the show listed on my résumé.

Christopher Seppe was so talented, I assumed that he would be getting bigger and better parts in New York. I wanted to be ready to take his place in *The Fantasticks*—or take the place of whoever replaced Christopher. So my senior year in college, I transferred to Armstrong State for one semester, so I could perform in Armstrong's production of *The Fantasticks*. That's when you know you have the theatre bug pretty badly—when you determine what college you will be attending by what shows their theatre departments are doing! After the semester was over, I transferred back to Valdosta State for the second semester and graduated.

Performing in the New York production of *The Fantasticks* became one of my major goals. I'm not proud to say it, but during this time, I offered many "bargaining prayers" to God. You know what I'm talking about—I promised to do something if God would do something. I really didn't think "bargaining prayers" worked—but I made them just in case they did! *The Fantasticks* was often the main subject of these prayers. These prayers went something like this:

"God, you know how much I would love to play the role of Matt in New York. I would give anything to do that role. In fact, I wouldn't have to do any other show for the rest of my life if I could do that one show. I would be fulfilled doing what Christopher Seppe does every night—playing Matt in *The Fantasticks* at Sullivan Street Playhouse. After I'm in the show for about three years, Lord, I promise that I'll do whatever you want me to do—go into the ministry—or whatever! *(pause)* Did you hear me, God? I wouldn't have to do another show. Just help me get this one—and that's it. You won't have to do another thing for me! Amen!"

After graduating from college I did summer stock again—this time in New Jersey at Glassboro State College. When the summer work was over, I moved to New York, hoping to audition for *The Fantasticks*. But then I found out that Christopher Seppe was still in the show. I couldn't believe it. Would he ever leave?

Then one day, I opened up *Backstage*, the newspaper that announces auditions for actors; and there in front of me was an article announcing auditions for *The Fantasticks*. I thought, "Yay! Christopher Seppe is finally moving on! Here's my chance!"

So I went down to Sullivan Street Playhouse in Greenwich Village for the audition. There, sitting at a table in front of me was none other than Tom Jones, who wrote *The Fantasticks* with Harvey Schmidt. What an honor it was, and a bit intimidating, to audition for one of the original authors of the legendary show. I felt that I gave a pretty good audition, but there were many other young men auditioning too. As I talked to some of them, I learned that Christopher Seppe was still in the show and that he was not planning on leaving. I did not understand. Why did they have auditions? They explained to me that every so often, the producers held auditions in order to keep their files filled with possible replacements, in case someone left the show. But Christopher Seppe did not have plans to leave. I was discouraged.

I continued to go to other auditions; and, as I mentioned in the previous story, I was fortunate to be cast as Frederic in *The Pirates of Penzance*. We rehearsed the show in New York, but performed it at Coachlight Dinner Theatre in Hartford, Connecticut. The show ran for two and a half months.

The way it worked at Coachlight is that the cast for their next show would rehearse in New York during the performance dates of their current show. Then, the cast of the next show would travel to Hartford to watch the last performance of the show currently playing. So when we had our last performance of *The Pirates of Penzance*, the cast of the next show was there to see us. The next show was to be the musical, *Whoopee!* So after our last performance of *Pirates*, the cast members of *Whoopee!* came up to our cast to meet us and congratulate us.

A young man came up to me and said, "Hi, my name is Chris Seppe, and I want you to know how much I enjoyed your performance."

I said, "Chris Seppe! Chris Seppe! I know you! I mean I know who you are! What are you doing here? You're not supposed to be here. You're supposed to be in New York!"

He said, "I'm in the cast of the next show here. I'm in *Whoopee!*"

"You can't be! You've got to be doing *The Fantasticks*! Because if you're not in the show, someone else is." I was also wondering why Chris would be doing a show in Connecticut when he could be doing a show in New York.

After I got over the initial shock that the person whose shoes I most wanted to be in was standing right in front of me, I had a nice conversation with Chris. It was very enlightening. Chris shared that he, of course, loved doing *The Fantasticks* in New York. But he also said he had been in the show for three years. Not only was he needing a change, the show had not led to any other jobs in New York. He felt he was getting stuck, and that he needed to move on. He also told me that since the theatre was so small in Greenwich Village—since it couldn't seat many audience members—the actors in *The Fantasticks* were paid very little. He said he was actually making more money at this new job in Connecticut than he was in the show in New York.

When I went back to my apartment that night to pack for the move back to Manhatten, I had to take some time to mull over what had just happened. I never dreamed I'd actually get to meet Christopher Seppe. I especially didn't think I would be meeting him in Connecticut. I never dreamed that instead of me going to where Christopher Seppe was, Christopher Seppe would be coming to me. And I never dreamed that we would have a meaningful conversation together.

Because Chris and I met in this strange, synchronistic

way, I learned that it was not the wisest thing in the world for me to think of being in *The Fantasticks* as my ultimate fulfillment in life. I learned that "bargaining prayers" are not a healthy way to relate to God. And I learned—well, I learned that I had a lot to learn!

Most of all, I learned that the best thing to do is to "Trust in the Lord with all your heart, and do not rely on your own insight. In all your ways, acknowledge him, and he will make your paths straight" (Proverbs 3:5-6).

The Tree

Epworth United Methodist Church in Savannah was my childhood church. From the time I was born until I went off to college, the people of Epworth nurtured and cared for me.

One of the members of the church was a man named Jack Byrd. Mr. Byrd worked for the Federal Bureau of Investigation. As a child, I thought it was really cool that we had an FBI agent at our church. I didn't think it was cool, however, when that FBI agent started dating my mother.

I'm afraid I didn't make courting my mother easy for Mr. Byrd. It had been just my mother, my sister, and me for a long time. It would be difficult for any fourth wheel to break into this deep-rooted trinity. Fortunately, Mr. Byrd was up for the task, which tells you he was a very patient and kind man. He and my mother married in April of 1972, when I was 12. Mr. Byrd, who became Jack the stepfather, turned out to be a great blessing to me and my family.

One of the blessings was financial. With Jack and his resources, we were able to move into a nicer home. We were able to travel more and do things we couldn't have done without him. Jack also was a blessing—emotionally and spiritually. A man of faith, Jack was a big part of our church.

He taught Sunday School and served on many committees. He was also a church historian. Jack and my uncle, Dr. Bob Hester, played a major role in getting a magnificent statue of John Wesley, the founder of Methodism, placed in one of the downtown squares of Savannah.

Jack especially lived out his faith as a caring stepfather. He attended my high school football games, purchased my first car, and helped me move to college. Most importantly, he was a steady and loving presence in my life. I couldn't have asked for a better stepfather and role model.

Jack was more practical than artistic. I know it was a stretch for him when I chose to pursue an acting career in New York City. Surprisingly, no one seemed happier than Jack when I landed my first lead role in New York. Perhaps it was because he knew the chances of making it in the acting profession were slim, so any kind of success was a big surprise and much to celebrate.

On September 11, 1982, just four days before I was to open in a lead role of *The Pirates of Penzance*, I got a call from my cousin, Phil Hunter, Jr. He had the horrible task of telling me that Jack had died in a boating accident. Jack and my Uncle Bobby had gone fishing in the waters of South Carolina that morning. Not far from the long bridge that connects Savannah and South Carolina are the towns of Bluffton and the more famous Hilton Head. By water, Bluffton and Hilton Head are very close to each other. It was in these waters that my uncle's boat struck something solid and unyielding. Both men were tossed out of the boat. My uncle barely survived before being rescued. Jack was not as fortunate.

As you might imagine, everyone was in shock. Here was

a man who had been a career FBI agent, who died suddenly while fishing. For me, the shock turned to anger. Jack had recently retired. He and my mother had just made the transition into their "enjoyment years." My mother had never had the opportunity to travel and see the world. She and Jack finally had the chance to do the things they'd like to do. Instead, she had to go through losing another husband in another unexpected, tragic way.

After I performed in *The Pirates of Penzance,* I went to Savannah to spend time with my mother. As I grieved Jack's death with her, I started going through my stepfather's materials and books. I stumbled upon something that took me by surprise. Jack had always been pleased by the fact that I was attending Marble Collegiate Church. He loved that I was having the opportunity to hear the great preacher, Norman Vincent Peale. But I had no idea just how much Jack admired Dr. Peale. As I went through Jack's files, I opened a folder that contained over 30 sermon pamphlets from the 1950s. They were old—antique looking—but in mint condition. He had obviously cherished them. On the front of each sermon was a drawing of a very familiar building. It was my New York church—Marble Collegiate. These were old sermons by Norman Vincent Peale. No wonder Jack was so happy about what I was experiencing in New York.

As I was spending time with my mother, I started to worry and be very concerned about her. How would my mother handle this death? What would happen to her? I understood there needed to be a period of time for depression and grief. But would my mother ever be able to rebound? A person can handle only so much stress. She had already had to overcome such tragedy once. Could she do it again? I was afraid that she would begin to shut down. Yet, she was only 53. She had so much of life ahead of her, but would she be able to pursue it? I made it my job to make sure she did. That was not a smart decision.

I became obsessed with fixing my mother. I kept encouraging her to do things—pushing her. Friends would tell me to relax—to give it time and trust the grieving and healing process. It will take time, they would say; but your mother will be fine. I didn't listen. Well I listened, but I didn't follow their advice. Part of me knew they were right, but I was so consumed by fear and worry that I couldn't resist pushing. Nothing anyone told me helped. I was starting to drive my mother crazy, my friends crazy, and myself crazy.

Fear and worry, as you know, can be very destructive. I knew that. I had been trained well by the attitude guru himself, Norman Vincent Peale. But I couldn't seem to do anything about it. I couldn't help it. And then came the dream.

I have never been good at remembering my dreams. I know there are people who dream dreams every night and can remember them in great detail. That's not me. But one night, I had a dream that Joseph would have been proud of!

There were only two subjects in the dream: a tree and myself. I was in the dream, and standing beside me was a large oak tree. The tree had a thick trunk and long branches, covered with green leaves. In the bark of the tree's trunk was a face—the face of my mother. The tree had my mother's features and expressions. I was amazed that a tree could look so much like a human being.

I was standing about seven yards from my mother, the tree. I waved one of my arms, gesturing to her to follow me. It was then that my mother, the tree, spoke. She said, "I can't."

I gestured to her again and said, "Come on! Follow me!" She leaned her trunk over and tried to pick up her long, deep roots so she could walk. But the roots would not come up.

I kept gesturing, and she kept trying, again and again. I could see that her straining to move was causing her pain—it's amazing how expressive a tree can be! Tears started rolling down her bark, and she said again, "I can't. It hurts." When I saw her tears and heard her voice this time, I stopped gesturing. It was painfully obvious that my mother needed to be right where she was.

The next morning, I felt like Ebenezer Scrooge waking up on Christmas Day! I was a changed man. The dream helped me realize that I was harming my mother more than helping her. People had told me that very thing, but it didn't help. No matter what people said or did, it didn't affect me. But when I saw it in a dream, I easily was able to change gears.

I no longer pushed my mother. I simply encouraged her to be wherever she needed to be. And it worked. Everyone was right. My mother would be fine. In time, she would go on all sorts of adventures—even walking across Central Park with me in a snow storm.

It's been 34 years, and my mother is still going strong at the age of 87. She is known for her incredible singing voice—a voice that shakes the rafters of the sanctuary during our services at Asbury Memorial—a voice from a strong woman with a strong faith—a faith as strong and solid as an oak.

Two Episcopal priests, Morton Kelsey and John Sanford, have both written extensively on the subject of dreams and spirituality. If you are interested in learning more about dream-work, I highly recommend their writings. One of Kelsey's books is titled *Dreams: A Way to Listen to God*. One of Sanford's is titled *Dreams: God's Forgotten Language*. Both Kelsey and Sanford would agree that you can have some wonderful wow moments (or "God moments") through your dreams.

Isn't it wonderful and amazing that God can help us even when we're not doing anything? God can bless us even when we are sleeping—even when we are dreaming of trees.

Plan B

This next story may not seem as "wowie" to you as it was for me. The power and mystery of what happened has a lot to do with what was going on internally with me at the time. After my stepfather's death in 1982, I started questioning my career choice.

As a young person, I was very active in three main areas: sports, theatre, and the church. All three were great passions of mine.

Like many young people, I had dreamed of playing professional sports. My hope of having an athletic career was short-lived. The only sport I had enough talent to pursue after high school was football. I had played linebacker for a state championship team. But during my years of blocking and tackling, I had about every tooth in my head knocked out. It didn't take long to realize that if I didn't want to visit an ER on a regular basis, I would need to move on to something else. So I did. My brain cells thanked me.

Theatre was next in line. After majoring in Theatre at college, I moved to New York in 1981. The following year I got a big break that I hoped would catapult my career. But soon after, my stepfather died tragically in a boating accident.

Since my birth father had died from a heart attack at the age of 35, I was already deeply aware of my mortality, frequently wondering about my family genes and the length of time I had on earth. My stepfather's death compounded those feelings. As I processed these thoughts, my passion for theatre began to fade. I felt that I needed to do something that helped people more directly. My experiences at Marble Collegiate Church confirmed my strong belief that a faith community can make a big difference in people's lives. So I considered going to seminary and into the ministry.

But the decision was not easy for me, especially since I was dealing with some good old-fashioned guilt. I had been taught not to be a quitter. I had invested time, energy, finances, and dreams into a theatrical career. I felt that if I changed gears, I would be letting my family and friends down. And I would be letting myself down. I had not achieved all I had wanted to achieve in the theatrical world, so my ego started playing games with me. For almost three years, I struggled with this decision, always with the same result: not letting go of theatre and not going to seminary.

1985 was a milestone year for Marble Collegiate Church. At the age of 86, Norman Vincent Peale retired as the senior minister, having served as head pastor for 52 years. His successor was Dr. Arthur Caliandro, who at age 51 had served as an associate minister at Marble for many years.

The stress of following in Dr. Peale's footsteps was immense. It was not long after taking the new position that Dr. Caliandro started having issues with his heart. In fact, he needed to have open heart surgery right away. The members of Marble Collegiate were concerned about their new senior minister. Fortunately, the surgery went well, and Dr. Caliandro was recovering in the hospital.

During this time, one of the associate ministers at Marble was a man named Jerry Everley. Jerry was from the South, loved sports, and happened to be United Methodist. He was designated as the church staff member who would relate to the members of The Actors' Fellowship group. Having a lot in common with Jerry, I soon developed a close relationship with him. He became my mentor. Seeing the great impact he had on my life and on the lives of many other people at Marble was another reason I wanted to go into the ministry.

One Sunday after a church service, Jerry came up to me and said, "Billy, could you do us a favor? Arthur is going to be discharged from the hospital this week. Would you mind helping him get home from the hospital? All you have to do is go to the hospital, get his luggage, and ride with him in a taxi to his Manhattan apartment."

I was a bit stunned. Why was Jerry asking me to help the senior minister of Marble Collegiate Church? There were many wonderful people at the church he could have asked. I did not know Dr. Caliandro very well. Many other parishioners knew him much better than I did. Surely Dr. Caliandro would prefer someone other than me—someone closer to him—to help him during this sensitive time.

Jerry continued, "Since you're an actor, I figured that your schedule is more flexible during the day than a lot of other people's. You think you can do it?"

"Of course," I said. "If it is okay with Dr. Caliandro, I would be honored to help."

So that week I went to the hospital and into Arthur's room. His wife, Gloria, was there, getting Arthur's things in order. Arthur was sitting in a wheelchair ready to go home. He looked weak, but he smiled and said how much he appreciated me coming. I took his luggage and went downstairs to hail the taxi that would take the three of us to their apartment. Arthur sat in the front seat of the taxi. After putting the luggage in the trunk, I sat in the back with Gloria.

As we rode down Fifth Avenue, Arthur turned in his seat as much as he could without popping his stitches and said, "So, Billy, how are you doing?" I was a bit caught off guard. I didn't expect the man who had just had open heart surgery to ask me how *I* was doing.

"Fine, thank you."

"How are things going with your career?"

"Well, to be honest, it's been challenging of late. It's been hard for me to get excited about auditioning and performing. I actually have thought about going into the ministry."

"That would be wonderful," said Gloria. "We need good people in the ministry."

Then I shared that it was hard for me to make a decision—that I couldn't seem to let go of theatre—that I felt like I was giving up. Then, Arthur said something I will never forget. "Billy," he said, "There's nothing wrong with having a Plan B. Everyone needs a Plan B."

His words did not convey some great philosophical statement, but for some reason, they connected with me in a powerful way. They were freeing—life-giving. Then Arthur said something that was just as amazing: "When we get to the apartment, come on up and let's talk about it."

Here was a man who had just had open heart surgery—who was just coming home from the hospital—who was willing to take the time to talk with me about my dilemma. I was amazed.

I left Arthur's apartment that day thankful—thankful that out of all of the members of Marble Collegiate, Jerry asked me to help Arthur and thankful that during his recovery, Arthur was willing to help me with this decision.

I soon applied to Princeton Theological Seminary and started attending classes in the fall of 1986. That taxi ride helped me make the decision to close the chapter of my theatrical career. Ironically, it was my theatrical career and my "flexible schedule" that gave me the opportunity to have the taxi ride with Arthur.

Eight years later in 1994, I called Arthur to get his advice on a church matter. I had been the pastor at Asbury Memorial for a year and wanted Arthur's opinion on one of our growing pains.

He said, "Billy, I happen to be coming down south to speak at an event in a couple of weeks. I think the town is only a couple of hours from Savannah. After the event, why don't I rent a car and drive to Savannah and spend some time with you. I can arrange it so that I fly back to New York from the Savannah Airport."

And that's what he did. Again, Arthur went out of his way to help me. He drove to Savannah after the event in South Georgia. We went out to lunch, and then we went to the church. As he sat in a pew on the first row, I couldn't believe Arthur was actually in my church in Savannah. I cherished this time of picking his brain about church matters. I felt infused and energized by his encouraging words. The next day he flew back to New York.

I didn't get to see or talk with Arthur too many times after that visit. But in 2011, a rather strange occurrence brought us together again. One afternoon five years ago, I was driving to a bank. That particular day I remember being bothered by something—a problem that I couldn't stop worrying about. As I pulled up to an ATM Machine, the name "Amelia Rossi" popped into my consciousness. When I say popped, I mean *popped*. I hadn't thought about Amelia Rossi in over 20 years. In fact, I couldn't believe that I remembered her last name—I had simply known her as "Amelia."

Who was Amelia Rossi? She was a close friend of Arthur's who had been a longtime member at Marble Collegiate. She lived to be 105 years old. Arthur would call and check on her every single day. He would take her out to lunch on her birthday. All of us had been inspired by Amelia's spunky spirit and longevity, but I had not thought of her since I left New York almost 20 years before. I couldn't believe that her name popped into my consciousness. "Where did that come from?" I wondered. "How did that happen? And why?"

The more I reflected on Amelia, the more I remembered the great admiration we all had for this little woman, who stood about five feet tall. Arthur would say she was a "bundle of positive energy." We were amazed at how she got around New York City at her age. She was the epitome of someone who lived in the moment and did not let fear or worry control her life. Even though she had lost two sons—even though she had been mugged on several occasions—she was fearless. Amelia said that for her the key to having a vibrant life is not to be afraid.

After having this rather mystical experience of Amelia and remembering her spunkiness and fearless faith, I was able to let go of what was weighing me down. Amelia's "visit" seemed to put everything in perspective.

Since Arthur and Amelia had been so close, I decided to write Arthur and tell him about my experience. I was a bit hesitant at first, concerned that Arthur might think that I had gone off the deep end. But Arthur often wrote and preached about mystical experiences—he was not shy about talking about experiences where there was an intersection of our earthly life with a higher realm.

He loved Teilhard de Chardin's quote, "We are not human beings searching for a spiritual experience; we are spiritual beings having a human experience." Surely Arthur would be open to hearing about this spiritual experience I had with his old friend. So I wrote him and told him about it. I was curious to see if he would write back.

Well, he didn't. He called me instead. About four days after I mailed the letter, Arthur called saying, "Tell me about your experience."

I shared that I was just driving, pondering over a problem; and, when I pulled into a parking lot, Amelia's name and image popped into my consciousness. I said to Arthur, "I don't understand it. I hadn't thought of Amelia for many, many years. I don't know how I remembered her last name. All I know is that after thinking about her, I was able to let go of what was bothering me."

"Thank you for sharing this, Billy. This means a lot to me," he said.

I mentioned to him that I planned to write a book about moments of wonder and synchronicity. I asked him if he would be open to writing the foreword for the book. He said, "I would be glad to do it for you, Billy." After all he had done for me, his response did not surprise me.

Unfortunately, I didn't write the book soon enough, because on December 30, 2012, Arthur made his transition. He was 79.

Since the man who helped me take the step into ministry couldn't write the foreword for the book, I decided not to include one. I guess we could say that was Plan B. It's always good to have a Plan B, you know.

The Dilemma

The two shows that dominated my musical theatre career were *Pippin* and *The Pirates of Penzance*. When I was in college, *Pippin* was one of the first musicals in which I got a lead role. Then I performed in a professional production of *Pippin*—the production in which I met my future wife, Cheri.

Pippin would come back into my life a third time.

After I had sent my application to Princeton Theological Seminary and had been accepted, a talent agent called to tell me about auditions for a revival of *Pippin* that would be coming to Broadway. He said the show would have its previews in Dallas, and then it would come to New York. If that wasn't exciting enough, he said the show would star and be directed by none other than Ben Vereen. The agent wanted to set up an audition for me.

Ben Vereen had been my idol! When I was a theatre major in college, I kept a picture of Ben Vereen on a wall in my dorm room. In 1972, Ben was nominated for a Tony Award for his role as Judas in the Broadway production of *Jesus Christ Superstar*. The following year, in 1973, he won the Tony Award for his portrayal of the "Leading Player" in the

Broadway production of *Pippin*. It was this role in *Pippin* that really put Ben Vereen on the map. And, of course, he later went on to play the unforgettable character of Chicken George in *Roots*, the celebrated miniseries on television in 1977.

The agent who called me with this information knew I had played the role of Pippin in two other productions. He wanted to send me to the audition for this revival, but I had already committed to attending Princeton. The timing would not allow me to do both. I had to choose one or the other.

My dialogue with God went something like this: "Lord, I know that I am planning to go to seminary. I want to be a minister. But it's Broadway, it's *Pippin*, and it's Ben Vereen! It's everything I've ever dreamed of. To perform the role of Pippin on Broadway playing opposite Ben Vereen would be one of the greatest highlights of my life. What should I do?"

I decided that since this was such a unique opportunity—since it was so coincidental—that perhaps I was meant to audition for the show. Besides, I knew that Princeton Seminary was not going anywhere. If I was in the show, I could still go to seminary afterwards. All I needed to do was defer to the following year. So I said: "Lord, if I get in this show, I promise that I will go to seminary right after *Pippin* is over."

I went to the audition, and there sitting at the table right in front of me was Ben Vereen. I remember trying to act normal, as though this was just like any other audition. But that was hard to do! Ben Vereen was right in front of me! After I sang, the production staff asked me to come back to another audition. Wow! I got a callback!

So I went back the next day for the callback, and they had me sing for them again. Then they gave me a script. They wanted me to read for them—to perform a scene from the show. After I did the reading, Ben Vereen stood up and came over to me. Then he put his arm around me as if I was his pal, and he started talking to me. I don't know what he said, because all I could think about was the fact that Ben Vereen had his arm around me. I think he put it there to try to help me relax. Little did he know that he was making my heart race faster and faster.

As we strolled together on the stage like old pals, my good buddy Ben started giving me stage directions and encouraging me to read the script a certain way. I knew it was impossible for me to give my best audition if I couldn't relax and be myself. But Ben Vereen was talking to me and had his arm around me! I don't think there was any way I could relax and act normal in that situation. It just wasn't going to happen. As a result, I didn't audition very well. I didn't get the part.

At first, I was pretty down about it. I couldn't understand it. It just seemed so right—as if the stars had lined up for me. But then came the new adventures at Princeton, and the world of seminary felt good and right. After three years of study, I graduated in 1989. Afterwards, I was hired as an associate minister at Marble Collegiate Church in New York.

❦

During the season of Lent, Marble Collegiate had a special program in their sanctuary called "Winter Wednesdays." Usually, the speakers at these services were public figures who were willing to share their faith journey.

On January 16, 1991, the title of the program was "Overcoming Adversity: The Triumph of the Human Spirit."

The prominent person coming to speak that night was none other than Ben Vereen. I couldn't believe it. Ben Vereen was coming to my church! I had not heard anything about Ben since the auditions for *Pippin* five years before. Apparently, the production of *Pippin* never made it to Broadway. It played outside of New York, but never made it back to "The Great White Way."

By the way, I remember the exact date Ben came to speak at Marble because, as he was speaking, we got word that Operation Desert Storm had begun; and Ben stopped his lecture to lead us in a time of silence and prayer.

Standing in a packed sanctuary, Ben openly and honestly shared how he had struggled in recent years. In 1987, his 16-year-old daughter, Naja, was killed tragically when a tractor-trailer tumbled over on a highway ramp in New Jersey, crushing the minivan she was in. Ben said he couldn't handle it. He fell into a deep depression. He developed a cocaine addiction. He entered rehab and struggled to regain his sobriety.

It has been said that religion is for people who don't want to go to hell, and that spirituality is for people who have already been there. Well, Ben Vereen had been to hell, and he was now focusing on his spirituality. He would still entertain people, but he was now more interested in speaking and sharing about important issues in life. He wanted to spend the rest of his life making a difference.

If I ever needed affirmation about my decision to go into the ministry, I got it that night. Oddly enough, I got it from the one person who could have delayed my entrance into the ministry. I got it from the man who, five years before, had his arm around me and held my future in his hands. Oddly enough, my theatrical idol had affirmed my new career.

Thanks, Ben, for having been a "Leading Player" in my life!

The Ring

Cheri and I married in New York City on June 27, 1987. We had a wedding ceremony at Marble Collegiate Church and a reception at the Princeton Club, where we were serenaded by a band that included the great, legendary jazz trumpeter, Doc Cheatham. There's a funny story about our experience with Doc, but that will have to wait until another book.

Cheri's generous parents were nice enough to foot the bill for the wedding and reception. They were not wealthy people. They had both been educators, but they had saved wisely. Plus, Cheri was an only child. Her parents would only have to pay this expense once.

Along with saving wisely, Cheri's parents also were great at finding deals, making investments, and getting airline mileage points. My resourceful in-laws somehow gave Cheri and me a honeymoon trip to Hawaii.

The trip started with some momentary setbacks that encourage young couples to bond together. My luggage was lost on the trip, and Cheri got a good case of sun poisoning. Things started looking up when we won a free helicopter ride—although that turned into a crazy adventure that should go in the same book with the Doc Cheatham story.

One of the highlights of the trip was a luau we attended. If you're not familiar with luaus, they are very large Hawaiian parties with lots of pineapple and pork. There are also lots of leis, grass skirts, and entertainment.

One of the purposes of a luau is to feast with people you do not know. You do not sit at separate tables as you would in a restaurant. You sit at long, picnic-like tables with strangers whom you hope will become friends. These celebrations are probably fun for extroverts, but challenging for introverts.

As we were passing the pineapple, pork, and poi around the table, I started up a conversation with the gentleman sitting on my right. He seemed pleasant and easy-going. As we shared our Hawaiian stories with each other, I could tell that he and his wife were having a good time.

That was not the case for the couple sitting directly across from us, who had hardly said anything. And when they said something to each other, it seemed to have a bit of sadness to it. They did not look happy.

Having my share of brawls with Cheri, I wondered what kind of argument these two had gotten into. Something had happened. I also wondered why they were there. If I was in a spat with my spouse, a luau is the last place I would want to be. In that environment, you are open—exposed to others. And everyone else is so happy, which would just make you feel worse. I suppose I should have been impressed that the couple attended the luau under the circumstances. But what were those circumstances, I wondered. Whatever struggle they were having, they decided to push through it.

As the man on my right and I continued to talk about

what we had been doing on the island, each of us shared that we had gone snorkeling—which is a popular thing to do in Hawaii. The man went on to tell me that while he had been snorkeling he found a man's wedding ring at the bottom of the ocean floor. He said that after he got back on the beach, he went to a lifeguard and asked him if anyone had lost a ring.

The lifeguard laughed and said, "Buddy, it happens all the time. People get married, come to Hawaii on their honeymoon, and are not used to having a ring on their finger. Then they go swimming or snorkeling, and the ring falls off, forever lost in the ocean." The lifeguard said there would be little hope of finding its owner.

As the man and I were talking, the woman sitting across the table from us apparently overheard our conversation. She said, "Excuse me. Did I hear you say that you found a wedding ring in the ocean today?"

"Yes," my new acquaintance replied, "I did."

The woman then extended one of her arms out in our direction, revealing a beautiful, expensive-looking ring on her ring finger. In a sad and sarcastic tone, she said, "It wouldn't happen to match this one, would it? My husband lost his in the ocean today."

Aha! That was the problem. The mystery was solved. That's why the couple was so down.

After the woman offered her sorrowful remarks, the man beside me looked at her ring. After a pause, he reached out and held the woman's hand so he could bend down and get a closer look at the ring. The man lifted his head and calmly said, "I have your husband's ring in my van." He got up from the table and said, "Let me go get it. I'll be right back."

Could it be? Could the ring he found really be the ring of the man sitting in front of us?

The man came back with a ring in his hand. He showed it to the couple, and they could not believe their eyes. It was the ring! None of us could believe it. Someone in charge of the luau heard what had happened and asked the two couples to come up on the stage, where they shared the story with everyone.

It was remarkable that the man found the ring in the first place. It was remarkable that both couples attended the same luau. It was remarkable that they happened to sit directly across from each other. It was remarkable that the man and I talked about snorkeling and that the man mentioned finding a ring. It was remarkable that the woman heard our conversation.

I've often thought how sad it would have been if all of those unique circumstances had come together, but the man and I had never talked to each other. Or what if we had talked, but he had never mentioned finding the ring? Or what if we had talked about the ring, but the couple wasn't sitting close to us to hear our conversation? All of the pieces would have been in place, but the ring would not have found its owner.

Remarkably, all of the pieces came together. And remarkably, the saddest-looking couple at the luau became the happiest-looking couple in Hawaii.

I regret that I did not get the names and contact

information of the two couples at the luau. If either of the couples happens to read this book, I would love it if they would get in touch with me. I realize that the chances are slim that they will ever come upon this story—but so were the chances of the husband ever getting his wedding ring back from the ocean.

Aloha!

THE BISHOP

In 1991, Cheri and I moved from New York to Savannah, Georgia, with our first child, Chelsea. I had the opportunity to serve as the associate minister at Wesley Monumental United Methodist Church. Since Cheri and I were new parents and were making the transition to the South, I thought it would be wise to spend a couple of years as an associate minister, instead of taking on the responsibilities that come with being a senior minister.

Wesley Monumental was a good choice. It was a large, beautiful church in historic downtown Savannah. The congregation was filled with wonderful people, many of whom became lifelong friends. The senior minister was an experienced and well-liked pastor named Hamp Watson. Hamp and his wife, Day, were a blessing to me and my family. Day will always be one of my heroes. She was badly stricken with polio as a teenager, yet was still able to complete college, complete graduate school, teach, and give birth to three children—not to mention be very involved in Hamp's ministry. She was amazing. Hamp was amazing, and they made an amazing team.

❦

But after two years as an associate minister at Wesley

Monumental, I was itching to try my hand at leading a congregation as the senior minister. I learned that the United Methodist denomination was planning to close a local church called Asbury Memorial. Growing up in Savannah, I remembered when Asbury Memorial was a thriving church with a vibrant congregation. It had been one of the strongest and most active churches in Savannah. But the 1960s, 70s, and 80s brought the white flight to the suburbs, and the urban church's membership declined.

To make matters more challenging, Asbury Memorial was located in a neighborhood that was designated by the City of Savannah as "Area C"—a low income, high crime neighborhood. On one side of the church was a condemned building that became a crack house. Directly behind the church was another house that also had illegal drug activity. You could get high just walking from your car in the parking lot to the door of the church. It wasn't unusual to hear gun shots ringing out during the night. On one occasion, the police chased a suspect all over Savannah and ended up shooting and killing him in the church parking lot.

By 1993, the congregation was so small that it could no longer afford a full-time minister. There were only 25 to 30 active members remaining, the youngest of which was 66 years old. The average age of the members was 80. Their part-time minister had encouraged them to start looking for another church to join since it looked as if Asbury would close. But the remaining members at "the Alamo" voted to stick it out to the bitter end.

When I heard about Asbury Memorial's situation, I was intrigued. I was interested in taking on the challenge and seeing what kind of ministry could be developed there. What did I have to lose? No one expected Asbury Memorial to grow, anyway.

❦

Even though I was interested in taking the job, I didn't *have* the job. In the United Methodist denomination, a minister doesn't apply for a job. He or she is appointed by a bishop. The bishop and his or her cabinet decide where to appoint each minister. The cabinet is made up of the various district superintendents in the conference.

My district superintendent at the time sounded very supportive of my desire to go to Asbury Memorial. I was encouraged by his willingness to explore this possibility. Unfortunately, the district superintendent does not have the final vote in the matter. The person who ultimately makes the decision is the bishop.

There were two things going against me. I learned that the bishop and his cabinet were considering me to serve another church in South Georgia. It was a newly-formed church, and they thought a fresh young minister would be ideal to lead the church into its future.

The second thing going against me was that many leaders in the denomination felt they had exhausted every avenue in trying to revive Asbury Memorial. The church started losing members in the late 1960s and had been on a steep decline ever since. Committee after committee had met for years to strategize about solving the "Asbury problem." Many different attempts were made to turn the tide in the 1970s and 80s. Nothing worked. Everyone was tired of trying to save Asbury Memorial. The feeling was that it was time to let it go.

Back to the bishop. The state of Georgia is divided into two United Methodist conferences: the North Georgia Conference and the South Georgia Conference. For many years, one bishop served both conferences. But in 1988, the denomination started doing something different. From then on, there would be two bishops in Georgia—one for the North Georgia Conference and one for the South Georgia Conference. For the first time, starting in 1988, the South Georgia Conference would have its very own bishop.

When a minister is elected to the position of bishop, he or she may not serve in his or her home conference. He or she must serve in a conference other than their own. So the first bishop of the South Georgia Conference would come from somewhere other than Georgia. The bishop who came to serve the South Georgia Conference in 1988 was a man named Richard Looney. Bishop Looney was from the Holston Conference, which is in Tennessee and Virginia. In order to have a chance of being appointed to Asbury Memorial, I would have to meet with the bishop and convince him that it was worth the effort.

This meeting with the bishop, however, wasn't as intimidating for me as it might seem. On the contrary, it was encouraging, because it seemed as though it had been ordained many years before.

Remember when I first moved to New York and started attending Marble Collegiate Church? Remember how I became part of a support group for actors called The Actors' Fellowship?

There was a young actress who came to The Actors' Fellowship named Teresa London. Teresa and I moved to New York at the same time. Both of us were from the South, and both of us were raised in the United Methodist denomination. We became close friends. In fact, like me, Teresa eventually would end up working on the staff at Marble Collegiate Church.

But Teresa London wasn't Teresa's real name. She had changed her last name for her theatrical career. Teresa's real name was Teresa Looney. Teresa London was Bishop Looney's daughter. Long before I met Bishop Richard Looney and long before he became a bishop and long before he moved to Georgia to be the first bishop of the South Georgia Conference, I became close friends with his daughter, Teresa.

You may remember me mentioning my good friend in New York, Rev. Jerry Everley, who was an associate minister at Marble Collegiate. Jerry was from the same conference as Bishop Looney—the Holston Conference. Jerry and his wife, Carolyn, were good friends of Richard Looney and his wife, whose name also happened to be Carolyn. In fact, Jerry was offered the job at Marble Collegiate because Richard had recommended him to Marble's senior minister, Arthur Caliandro.

When I was ordained as a United Methodist minister in 1989 in Macon, Georgia, I asked Jerry if he could attend the ordination service and place the ministerial stole on me. He agreed to do so. Jerry and Carolyn drove all the way to Macon for the service—a service that their good friend Bishop Richard Looney presided over. So Jerry and Carolyn not only got to see Cheri and me, they got to spend time with their old friends, Richard and Carolyn Looney.

I first met Bishop Looney one summer when he came to New York to be a guest preacher at Marble Collegiate Church. I met him again when he came to New York to see his daughter, Teresa. I also got to see him again when he came back to New York to walk Teresa down the aisle at her wedding. This all happened before Rev. Richard Looney became Bishop Looney.

So even though the odds were stacked against me to be appointed as the minister at Asbury Memorial, there seemed to be a Greater Spirit at work. Because of the past history I had with the first bishop of the South Georgia Conference who came from the Holston Conference, I knew there was a possibility that he would give Asbury Memorial one more chance. And thankfully, he did.

The revitalization of Asbury Memorial and the development of its vibrant ministry have been made possible by a lot of hard work, a lot of prayer, a lot of creativity, a lot of faith, and a lot of commitment by a lot of people. I am especially grateful for the hard work and the hopeful spirits of the members of Asbury Memorial. They are the reason the church has once again become a strong and caring congregation. But we might never have had the opportunity to be a strong congregation again had the first bishop of the South Georgia Conference not been Richard Looney, the guest preacher at Marble Collegiate Church, the good friend of Jerry Everley, and most of all, the father of Teresa London.

BUTCH

In many ways I had a storybook childhood. That sounds strange for me to say, since my father died when I was four years old. My father's sudden death from a heart attack at the age of 35 certainly caused great heartache and difficulties for my family. But there were so many other ways we were blessed.

I was fortunate to have a wonderful mother and older sister. The three of us had a host of nurturing relatives on both sides of our family, who were always there for us. We also were fortunate to have a supportive church family. We lived in a great neighborhood and had many friends. We were blessed!

There was one other reason that I felt extra-blessed. I was the luckiest kid in the world because I had an incredible cousin named "Butch."

Butch was 18 years older than me. After my father's death, Butch took it upon himself to be my big brother, coach, and best friend. Butch not only became a mentor for me, he became the Pied Piper for all of the kids in my neighborhood.

My earliest memory of Butch was not a pleasant one. I got upset and refused to say goodbye to him. I was four or five at the time, and he was in the last year of serving as a medic in the Army. He had come home for Christmas, and he came over to our house to see all of the relatives while he was on leave. The evening had gotten late, and it was time for Butch to go. He would be heading back to his military duties the next day.

I was scared that I would never see him again. My father had just died, and Butch was in the army. As a four-year-old, I assumed he would be going off to war and would not be coming back. So I locked myself in a back bedroom refusing to say goodbye—as though that would keep Butch from leaving. People called and called for me to come out of the room. I wouldn't budge.

After Butch and the other relatives finally gave up trying to coax me out of the room, I heard footsteps walk away and the front door of the house open and close. Butch was gone. I opened the bedroom door and ran to the front of the house as fast as I could.

With tears streaming down my face, I looked through a window into the darkness, seeing only shadows of people on the front lawn and Butch's car pulling away from the curb. I knocked on the glass and shouted, "Goodbye," only to have my voice fall on deaf ears. Butch was gone. It was one of the worst nights of my life.

Fortunately, Butch would eventually come back home. He completed his military duties and returned to Savannah. I was ecstatic.

From that time on until the day I left for college, Butch would come over to my house at least once a week after he got off work from his job at Roberds Dairy. Would it be Friday or Saturday? Would it be 4:30? 5:00? 5:30? How long would he be here? How much time would he spend with us?

Every Friday and Saturday, the kids in the neighborhood would peek out of their windows to see if Butch's car was parked in front of my house on the corner of 65th Street and Abercorn. If the car was there, children would flock to our house as if the ice cream truck had arrived.

Then we would play football, baseball, basketball, a board game, or go see a movie. If we were lucky, when it got late, we would go outside in the dark; and Butch would tell some of his famous ghost stories. From all of these experiences, Butch taught us about comradery, integrity, perseverance, bravery, courage, laughter, and all the things that young people should learn and experience. It was magical!

I always knew that we were blessed to have Butch in our lives, but I never realized just how incredible Butch was until I became a parent and tried spending quality time with my children while holding down a job. Butch had done it masterfully.

If any of the kids in the neighborhood were struggling with something, Butch was always there for us. He did his best counseling in his car. We'd sit in the parked car in front of the house, talking things over. When it looked like the conversation was coming to an end, Butch would turn the key and crank up the engine, only to shut it off again when he realized more needed to be discussed. This process could go on for over an hour.

Butch and I both loved sports and movies. Through these

two venues and their stars, we talked about important things in life: the hard work ethic of Colts' receiver Raymond Berry, the cool composure of Johnny Unitas, the consistency of Bart Starr, the toughness of John Wayne. We especially loved the film, *Butch Cassidy and the Sundance Kid*. He was Butch, and I was the Kid.

The only thing Butch and I did not do together was church. Butch was Roman Catholic, and I was Methodist. He was a huge Notre Dame fanatic (with a capital "F"). Butch was so enamored with the Fighting Irish that you would have thought his father was Knute Rockne. I had fun pulling for whatever football team Notre Dame was playing against, just so that I could give Butch a hard time. Of course, in those days, Notre Dame's football teams were very good—they almost always won.

The only time Butch and I saw a live Notre Dame game together was in November of 1976, when they played Georgia Tech in Atlanta. Somehow, the lowly Tech team upset the mighty Irish. The only solace Butch could find from the humiliating loss was the fact that the quarterback for Georgia Tech was Gary Lanier, a childhood friend of mine and former teammate from Savannah. Gary was a master at running the triple-option. He rarely threw a forward pass. In fact, he is the only quarterback to beat Notre Dame without throwing a single pass the entire game. Gary had played quarterback at Butch's former Catholic high school, Benedictine. Butch loved his Benedictine Cadets! So all was not lost since Notre Dame had been beaten by a Cadet.

One of the hardest things about going off to college and moving to New York was being separated from Butch. I was thrilled when he was willing to come up to the Big Apple to be my best man for Cheri's and my wedding in 1987. Four years later, in 1991, we would decide to move to Savannah. After being away for 14 years, Butch and the Kid would be together again.

Cheri and I had been in Savannah for over a year when, on a January night in 1993, I awoke from a deep sleep due to a ringing telephone. I looked at a clock. It was midnight. I had dozed off in a chair while watching the news. Since it was so late, I knew the phone call must be important. I tumbled out of the chair and hurriedly picked up the phone. It was Butch.

"Billy," he said, "I think I'm having a heart attack."

"I'll call 911," I said. "If the ambulance beats me to your house, I'll see you at the hospital!"

I hung up the phone and dialed 911. After giving the information to the dispatcher, I called two childhood friends who were close to Butch and asked them to meet me at his house. Even though we got to Butch's as fast as we could, the ambulance had come and gone. The sheets on Butch's bed had been practically torn away from the mattress, revealing that he had had a restless and painful night.

The three of us rushed to the hospital, wondering if Butch was still alive. We went to the emergency room, where we were pleased to find Butch conscious and talking. He looked uncomfortable on the stretcher, but he was able to speak. The doctor wanted to do a heart catheterization.

As they were rolling him into the operating room, Butch looked at the three of us and said, "If this is it, fellas, I want you to know that I love you."

I said, "Butch, don't worry. You'll be okay." Then they rolled him away.

Unfortunately, something went terribly wrong during the procedure. Butch would not wake up and was put into the Intensive Care Unit. With no spouse or children or living siblings, Butch's closest relatives were his cousins. The doctor communicated to us that Butch's prognosis was not good and that he was on life support.

A couple of days went by, and there had been no change. Nothing we said or did was waking Butch up. If things did not change soon, the doctors would encourage us to take Butch off life support. There was only one thing I could think of that might make a difference: "The Notre Dame Fight Song." If "The Notre Dame Fight Song" wouldn't wake Butch up, nothing would.

So I rode to every music store in Savannah trying to find a recording of it (this was before the Internet). I finally found the song and got a small cassette player and headed to the hospital. I went to Butch's room where two nurses and my cousin John surrounded the bed. I placed the cassette player beside Butch's head and turned it on. The music started. "Cheer, cheer for old Notre Dame. Wake up the echoes cheering her name. Send a volley cheer on high. Shake down the thunder from the sky...." The music continued to play.

I wish I could tell you that Butch woke up. Unfortunately, that didn't happen. But something almost as amazing did—or perhaps it was even more amazing. During the playing of the "Fight Song," Butch's pulse slowed. It kept slowing and slowing and then stopped after the song had played for about two minutes.

I could hear sniffling and saw tears from the nurses gathered in the room. In all my years of ministry and being with people dying, I've never seen nurses cry so openly in a hospital room. It looked like a scene from a movie—like out of the Knute Rockne story or something—just the way my sappy cousin Butch would have wanted it.

The following day Cheri and I were to meet with a therapist. We were having some marital challenges, and we found meeting with this psychologist to be helpful. But I was a mess. Having spent so much time with Butch at the hospital, I had gotten little sleep for three days. I was in the middle of trying to plan Butch's funeral. As the executor, I had to make the burial arrangements and make payments. I would also be writing a eulogy that I would deliver at his funeral.

So as Cheri and I sat down with the therapist, I was exhausted and overwhelmed. I found it impossible to focus on Cheri's and my issues. We soon discovered that there was something else going on. I was feeling guilty—terribly guilty.

As the therapist supplied questions, I began to share that I had messed up. When I was in the emergency room with Butch, the last thing he said to me and the other guys was, "If this is it, fellas, I want you to know that I love you." I wished I had said, "Butch, if this is it, I want you to know that we love you, too. And thank you for all you have done for us!" But I didn't. Instead, I told him everything would be okay. Butch had been awake and talking to us. People have catheterizations all the time. I didn't think there would be a problem.

More importantly, I didn't want to upset Butch. I wanted him to feel calm and positive as he went in for surgery. Had I known that it was the last time I would see him, I would have told him that I loved him.

The therapist said, "Billy, don't you know that he knows you love him? He can hear you now."

In a frustrated tone, I said, "But I want to see his face! I want to see his face when I tell him."

It wasn't until the writing of this manuscript that I realized the profound connection of this moment with my first memory of Butch—the night I refused to say goodbye to him. Here it was thirty years later, and I had messed up saying goodbye to him again. And this time, Butch was not coming back.

There were no easy answers for my pain and frustration, but sharing my feelings with the therapist and with Cheri did me a world of good. I felt better. It was if a load had been lifted from my shoulders. Something transforming had happened through the sharing of these deep emotions.

As I left the office of the therapist and got into my car, I turned the key and cranked up the engine. The radio came on. A commercial was playing that featured a man with a rather brassy voice that was a bit annoying. I started to change the station. When I put my finger on the radio controls, I realized there was a familiar tune playing underneath the man's words as he spoke. It was a happy and upbeat tune. I liked it, but I couldn't place the song. So I started humming along with it to see if, by humming it, I would be able to recognize it.

After humming about ten notes, it dawned on me that the song I was listening to was "The Notre Dame Fight Song." I couldn't believe it. I had never heard the song on the radio before, and I have never heard it since.

I wondered if Butch was letting me know that everything was okay. I wondered if he was doing a little more counseling in the car. I wondered if he was letting me see his face.

Cheer, cheer for old Notre Dame,
Wake up the echoes cheering her name.
Send a volley cheer on high.
Shake down the thunder from the sky!

Dix

The church I pastor in Savannah is known for being a welcoming, inclusive congregation. Asbury Memorial almost closed in the early 1990s. One reason the church is now thriving again is because of our lesbian, gay, bisexual, and transgender (LGBT) members. They have been some of our most committed and hardest workers. For example, we have a lesbian couple who lived in Jesup, Georgia, and drove 67 miles to church every Sunday with their children. They recently moved closer to Savannah. Now they live in Statesboro and only have to drive 56 miles each way!

The fact that I am the pastor of a congregation that consists of a large number of LGBT people is quite remarkable. Like many people of my generation, I grew up being taught that homosexuality was wrong. More than that, it was a sin. People "like that" needed to change, or they would experience eternal damnation. This was not the message I received from my mother, who raised me to have compassion for everyone. But it is the message I received from the church and from the culture that surrounded me.

Homosexuality wasn't something I heard much about as

a child in the 1960s. The first recollection I have of seeing an openly gay person was when I was 12 in 1972. My mother had remarried, and we moved to a new neighborhood. My grandmother moved into our old house on 65th Street between Abercorn and Habersham Streets. Since most of my friends were in my old neighborhood, I would often go to 65th Street to see them and to spend time with my grandmother.

On one such visit, my friends said that "two men" had moved into our neighborhood—two men from New York! Two men from the city of heathenism had moved onto our block! How dare they? What was the world coming to? We couldn't believe this was happening in our neighborhood!

I never met either of the men. My friends and I spied on them from afar, as though they were aliens from outer space. They were the brunt of many of our jokes—jokes which included words like "queers," "queens," and "fags." "Thank God we were not like them!" we thought.

Homosexuality became a more prominent issue for me when I was in college. I was a Theatre major and a number of people in our department were gay. Most of them seemed genuinely nice. They were just misguided, I thought. I tried to "love the sinner, but hate the sin."

There was one fellow, however, who made me do some thinking. His name was Ken. Not only was he funny and fun to be around, Ken was one of the most honest and authentic persons I had ever known. Ken did not attend church, but there was something really good about him. There was also something about Ken that seemed a little different. I thought he might be gay. He never talked about it. He and I could talk about anything and everything—except that subject. I felt awkward asking him if he was gay. What if he wasn't? Would it make him feel bad that I thought he appeared gay? So I kept waiting for Ken to talk with me about his sexual orientation. He never did.

My senior year in college, Ken and I decided to share an apartment off campus. I was still thinking about having the "gay talk" with him, but a strange thing started happening. Ken would sometimes not come home at night. When I questioned him about it, he told me that he was spending the night with a woman. In fact, he had been spending lots of nights out with several different women. I could not understand it. What was Ken thinking? This was not healthy for him, and it was not healthy for the women he was seeing. And it sure blew my whole theory about Ken being gay.

A couple of years later, I was dating my future wife, Cheri. She was performing in a touring production of *Joseph and the Amazing Technicolor Dreamcoat* in Boston. Ken was living in Boston at the time, so I took a trip to see Cheri and Ken. I told Cheri, "This is silly. Ken and I have always been honest about everything. I'm not leaving Boston without asking him if he is gay."

As Cheri was performing in a matinee, Ken and I got together. As we were walking down a Boston street, I took a deep breath and said, "Ken, there is something I've wanted to ask you for a long time."

Before I could say another word, Ken said, "Yes, I am." We both laughed.

Ken shared with me that during college, he thought he

was gay; but he didn't want to be. So he kept trying to sleep with women to prove that he was straight. It didn't work, of course. I began to understand some of the pain that many gay people suffer. I began to start questioning some of my preconceived notions about homosexuality, especially the belief that one's sexual orientation was a choice.

I learned another great lesson from Ken. He told me that he had wanted to share with me that he was gay; but he was afraid that if he did, he would lose my friendship. I cared deeply for Ken, and it hurt me to know that he thought I might dissolve our friendship because of his sexual orientation.

When I moved to New York and started attending Marble Collegiate Church in 1981, I met people at church who were openly gay. I had never experienced this before. Not only were they openly gay Christians, they were leaders in the church. It was also the first time that I met gay couples who had been together 10, 20, 30 years, or more. As I got to know these men and women, I discovered that they were people of great integrity. One couple in particular, Stuart and Gary made a huge impression on me. They were dedicated Christians with loving hearts who loved their Lord. My preconceived notions and assumptions about gay people kept being shattered.

I also met LGBT people who were struggling to accept themselves and their sexual orientation. Many of these people had been raised in the South and in fundamentalist religion. They had been taught that homosexuality was an abomination—that *they* were an abomination. They felt so bad about themselves that they were willing to do anything to change.

Some of them went to prayer and healing services, hoping to be healed of what they considered to be an affliction. When that didn't work, some of them turned to alcohol. Others attempted suicide. The Christian church had not helped these people. It had caused them harm. Something was terribly wrong.

Then there was AIDS. New York was a challenging place to live in the 1980s during the start of the AIDS epidemic. People with AIDS were modern-day lepers, like the lepers who were rejected and abandoned during the days of Jesus. Fortunately, I was blessed to be part of a church community in New York that offered love and acceptance to people living with AIDS. But it wasn't that way at most churches.

I will never forget the first time I went to a hospital as a minister to visit a person who had AIDS. When I found his room, the door was shut. In large print on the door were the words, "Caution: Must wear gown, gloves, and mask."

"Oh my goodness" I thought, "Can I catch something?" Cheri and I had just had our first child. I was concerned that I could carry the disease back to Cheri and my infant daughter.

I saw a nurse and said to her, "Do I really need to wear all of this?" The way I asked her, I tried to make it sound like I didn't want to make the patient feel strange; but I was really asking so I could find out how contagious he was.

"Yes," she said, "you *do* need to wear them. We want to make sure he doesn't catch something you may be carrying." Yes, of course. *His* immune system was compromised. *He* had to be protected—from *me*!

❦

During my studies at Princeton Theological Seminary, I learned that the Christian church—since its very beginning—has always struggled with change and being more accepting and inclusive of others. Gentiles, for instance, were not to be accepted as Christians unless they followed all of the Law of Moses. That's what the "Bible said"—which was only the Hebrew Scriptures at the time. But the apostle Paul encouraged the early Christians to see that this wasn't the will of God—that it wasn't the loving thing to do. It was a huge controversy that reshaped the Christian Church at its very beginning.

My own denomination split in 1844 over slavery. It became the Methodist Episcopal North and the Methodist Episcopal South. Members of the Methodist Episcopal South used passages in the Bible that affirmed slavery to rationalize their position of hate and oppression. It seems unfathomable to us today.

The church did the same thing regarding the oppression of women. The Bible was written in a patriarchal culture that did not hold women in high regard. For instance, Paul wrote that women were to remain silent in the church. It wasn't until 1956 that women were allowed to become ordained ministers in the Methodist denomination.

I had always taken the Bible at face value—being in denial about its inconsistencies and the parts that did not resonate with the spirit of Christ. I learned that there is a difference between the Word of God and the words of God. God did not dictate the 66 books that are in the Bible. People wrote them—

wrote them out of their own experiences and reflections in a particular culture and context. Yes, the words are inspired. Yes, there is truth. But there is still a human element. Paul, for instance, thought Jesus was going to return soon—perhaps in his own lifetime. When we read that Moses ordered all the women and children to be killed, his actions do not match up with the teachings of Jesus. I could make a long list of the Bible passages and stories that don't resonate with the spirit of Christ.

John Wesley, the founder of Methodism, was well aware of these inconsistencies. Even though parts of the Bible affirmed slavery, he strongly opposed it. The last letter he wrote before he died was to William Wilberforce, a member of Parliament, encouraging Wilberforce to continue fighting against slavery. I've always found it interesting that the Methodist Episcopal South supported slavery, even though the founder of Methodism did not.

Since Wesley knew that knowing the will of God could be challenging, he encouraged people to use four sources to discern God's will: Scripture, Tradition, Experience, and Reason. These resources are four gifts given to us by God to help and guide us. But it takes study and effort. In other words, I had been a "lazy Christian"—not wanting to do the work—not wanting to wrestle with the issues.

While at Princeton, I wrote a research paper on "Homosexuality and the Bible" in an ethics class taught by Dr. Peter Paris. I discovered that just as people had been indoctrinated with racism and misogyny, they had been indoctrinated with homophobia. The Bible was being misused against LGBT people, just as it had been misused against African-Americans and women.

During my work on this paper, I had an incredible wow moment. One of the major resources I used for my research was *The Church and the Homosexual*, a book by John McNeill. In fact, I used several books written by John McNeill for the paper. McNeill was a brave pioneer on the subject of homosexuality and the church. He had been ordained a Jesuit priest in 1959, but was expelled in 1987 because of his views on homosexuality and his work with gay people.

He then became a psychotherapist. His books were among the first to offer support for LGBT people in the faith community. Since social justice issues were becoming more important to me, McNeill became one of my heroes. A wow moment came when I asked a colleague at Marble Collegiate, associate minister Rev. Rob Williams, if he had ever heard of John McNeill.

Rob said, "Heard of him? He works in our building. He's a therapist at the counseling center above us." Our offices were on the second floor of a high rise the church owned at 3 West 29th Street, and the church leased the fourth and fifth floors to a counseling center. Out of all the places in this world, John McNeill and I worked in the very same building. John McNeil was right above me! Incredible!

Not long after the conversation with Rob, I got to meet John McNeill. Rob asked him to be the featured speaker at an event for one of our church groups. How wonderful it was to meet the person I had used as a major resource for my research paper—a man who had sacrificed greatly for the rights of homosexuals.

❦

When I moved back to Savannah in 1991, I returned with a very different understanding and theology concerning homosexuality. After accepting the position as senior minister at Asbury Memorial, it was important for me to help create a church environment where all people felt welcomed and accepted. But it's hard to welcome and accept people if there are no people to welcome and accept. The church was on the verge of closing. There were only 25 to 30 active members, and the youngest member was 66 years old.

Another challenge facing the church was its neighborhood. The City of Savannah deemed it "Area C"—a high crime, low income neighborhood. Many Savannahians considered it to be a very dangerous area. How in the world would we get people to come to church so we could welcome and accept them?

The only thing I knew to do that would draw people was to create a community theatre. We would produce two musicals a year. We would have open auditions—anyone in Savannah could audition. Maybe, if we cast someone in a show, they would build relationships with other people at Asbury and become part of our faith community. Also, we hoped that the people who came to see the shows would try attending the Sunday worship services.

In order to get Savannahians to come to what they thought was our "scary neighborhood," the productions would have to be really good. The first production was *The Pirates of Penzance*—a show I knew backwards and forwards since I had performed it in New York. Our production got very good reviews. The word spread, and people came. It played for two weeks, to standing room only audiences.

The only negative news that came out of this first production was that Nathan Heverin, the young man who designed and built the set for the show, was leaving Savannah. Nathan was an excellent craftsman and set designer. He, however, wanted to study set design professionally and make it his career. So soon after our first show, Nathan moved from Savannah. By the way, Nathan did "make it" as a set designer in New York. He has done very well in show business. We were happy for Nathan, but now the inner city theatre-church was without a set designer.

Soon after our first show, an older man named Dix Elliott visited the church one Sunday. The 73-year-old dressed immaculately and carried himself with a bit of flair. He had a gruff sounding voice, the result of way too many cigarettes. Dix came up to me after the worship service and shared that, as he was sitting in the pew, he felt his mother's presence. He said he felt as though he had come home. Dix wanted Asbury to be his church. He mentioned that he used to be a fashion designer in New York and that he had retired to Savannah. He also mentioned that he had done a lot of work with scenic design and scenery painting. He asked if we needed any help with the next show.

I said, "You've got the job!"

I wasn't sure where this mysterious stranger had come from—like an angel appearing out of thin air. Dix Elliott was an answer to prayer. For the next eight years, Dix created magic on the church Social Hall stage. In one of the poorest areas of Savannah, he created professional-looking, artistic sets that helped us produce wonderful shows—shows that drew people from all over the Southeast to "Area C" of Savannah.

Dix became one of my closest friends. He was gay and was very honest and open about his sexual orientation. In fact, he had participated in the famous Stonewall uprising in Greenwich Village in 1969—one of the most important events leading to the gay liberation movement.

I never knew Dix's partner, John, who had died many years earlier. Dix gave me a large, haunting rendition of the crucifixion of Jesus that John had painted. I keep this treasure in my office.

Dix lived alone, but had many friends. Between his faith community and his theatre community, he was much-loved and supported.

Dix was born in Augusta, Georgia. As a young man, he wanted to go to seminary at Duke to become a minister. But he was well aware of his sexual orientation, and he knew there was no future for him in the church. So Dix moved to New York and became a reputable fashion designer with his partner, John. We were blessed that Dix moved to Savannah and found Asbury Memorial. He played a major part in the revitalization of the church. I will be indebted to him forever.

During the time he created his artistic masterpieces for our theatrical productions, Dix was battling cancer. He would have horrible coughing fits as he was stretched out on the Social Hall floor painting large flats. I would tell him to stop painting and rest, but he'd say, "I'd be happy to die right here, doing what I love to do and being where I want to be—at my church."

❦

Not long after Dix became a member of Asbury, one of our musicals opened with his great scenic backdrops. When he arrived at the church for the performance, he said, "Billy, my car has broken down. Someone gave me a ride to the church. Do you think you could give me a ride home after the show?"

"Of course," I said. "Be glad to."

When the show was over, we got in the car and I said, "Dix, I should know this, but where is it that you live?"

"Oh," he said, "I live on 65th Street, between Habersham and Abercorn."

"Oh really?" I said. "That's funny. I used to live on that same street when I was a child."

As I was driving and getting closer to 65th Street, something dawned on me that sent chills down my spine. Could it be? If Dix lives on my old street, could he actually be one of the "two queers" that had moved from New York City into my neighborhood when I was a teenager? Could Dix be one of the men that my friends and I had made fun of and called names over 20 years ago? My heart began to pound.

As we approached 65th Street, Dix started to tell me which house was his, so I would know where to park. Before he got three words out of his mouth, I said, "Dix, you don't need to tell me. I know *exactly* where you live." Dix and John were indeed the two men I had made fun of and ridiculed.

I spent many more hours on 65th Street—not outside of Dix's house, calling him names or laughing at him. These hours were spent *inside* his house, talking with Dix and laughing *with* him—and thanking him for what he did for me and for God's Church.

Dix died on April 30, 2003. We had a wonderful celebration of his life at Asbury Memorial. Afterwards, we got into our cars and caravanned to Augusta, Georgia, for his service of interment in a local cemetery.

I learned from Dix's obituary that he had been in the Battle of the Bulge and had received the Purple Heart. I also learned that he and his partner John founded The Court Jester of Fashion Design in New York City—which is ironic, since the logo for Asbury Memorial is a clown that looks very much like a court jester (a long story for another book).

Dix remembered his church in his will and left a significant financial gift that has blessed many people. I am so thankful for the day Dix Elliott came to Asbury Memorial. I'm so thankful that he felt his mother's presence in our sanctuary, letting him know that he was home. I'm so thankful he became my friend.

Not a Sunday goes by that I don't feel Dix's presence at Asbury. Not a Sunday goes by that I don't give thanks for the gay man who moved to 65th Street, between Habersham and Abercorn.

THE SCAR

When I started my ministry at Asbury Memorial in 1993, the congregation was so small that they could not afford to pay the salary for a full-time minister. So I also pastored another church, Wesley Oak United Methodist Church. Wesley Oak could not afford a full-time minister either, so I served both churches as a part time minister.

During this time, I was under a great deal of stress because both Asbury Memorial and Wesley Oak were on the verge of closing. I was trying my best, not only to keep both churches open, but to help them grow.

There was another major stress factor in my life. While serving both churches, Cheri and I were the parents of a five-year-old daughter, a three-year-old daughter, and twin newborn sons. Yikes!

After serving both churches for seven years, I was at my wit's end. My training from my days back at Marble Collegiate Church kicked in and said, "Billy, you need help in dealing with this stress. You need to be in therapy."

Cheri and I were seeing a therapist for our marriage at the time, but it was clear that I also could benefit from individual counseling. I asked our marriage therapist if she had suggestions for someone for me to see. Since I was fairly well-known in the Savannah community, I felt more comfortable about issues of confidentiality if the therapist was outside of Savannah, in one of the surrounding communities. Our therapist told me that she had heard good things about a psychologist named Paul Doerring, who practiced on Hilton Head Island.

Hilton Head is about a 45-minute drive from Savannah, so I told her that sounded perfect. Not only would I benefit from Dr. Doerring's counseling, I would enjoy some time in the car alone, especially since the drive included scenic views of marsh and water. So I started seeing Dr. Paul Doerring, who was a wise sage and exactly what I needed at that time in my life.

If the door to Dr. Doerring's office was closed when I arrived, it meant that he still had a patient with him so I would wait in the lobby until he finished. If his office door was open when I arrived, I was to go right on in and start my session.

One day in 2000, I arrived about ten minutes early. The door was closed, so I sat in the waiting area. After I selected a magazine to read while I waited, two young girls entered the building and sat down in the waiting area with me. The older girl looked to be about 12, and the younger girl looked to be about 10. Because of the way they related to each other and because of their physical similarities, I assumed they were sisters.

I sat there pretending to read the magazine—pretending because I became concerned that Dr. Doerring had double-booked his calendar. The door to Dr. Doerring's office was usually open when I arrived. And on the few occasions that the door was closed, no one had been in the waiting room with me. Were these young girls also waiting to see Dr. Doerring? Had I gotten the wrong day for my appointment?

As these thoughts were crossing my mind, I heard the younger girl say, "How did you get that?"

The other girl—her big sister—did not answer her.

I looked up from the magazine to see what the little girl was talking about and to see why her sister did not respond. To my surprise, the little girl was looking at me. Her question, "How did you get that?" was directed to me.

"I'm sorry," I said, "How did I get what?"

The girl pointed to her neck. "That!" she said.

I had recently had neck surgery that left a Frankenstein-like scar on the front of my neck. It would eventually disappear, but on this day it was still quite visible and scary-looking. I had worn a button-down shirt so that I could keep my collar open. The open collar would not rub against the fresh scar, but it also made the scar more visible.

But why would a little girl be asking a stranger how he got a scar on his neck?

I pointed to my neck and said, "Do you mean this?"

She said, "Yes. How did you get it?"

I was a bit surprised. When I was a child, I never would have asked a complete stranger how they got a scar. She hadn't even said, "Hello." Just, "How did you get that?"

After I recovered from the boldness of this "Mighty Mouse," I said, "Well, I had neck surgery. I had a bad pain in my neck, so I had to have an operation."

"Oh," she said. "I got mine from a dog."

"You've got a scar?" I asked.

"Two of them," she said. "A smaller one on this side of my face." She pointed to her cheek. Sure enough, there was a small scar that I had not noticed. "And," she said, "I've got a bigger one on this side." She turned her head so I could see the other side of her face. I was stunned. There was a long scar from the top of her cheekbone all the way down to the bottom of her chin.

The light bulb came on. The little girl's question, "How did you get that?" was not the question of a nosy child. It was the question of someone who had a shared experience—someone who had a shared, *difficult* experience.

With some help from her big sister, the little girl went on to tell me that a neighbor's dog had attacked her—a dog she had been around a hundred times before. But, for some reason on this occasion, the dog got spooked—it turned on the child and attacked her.

The plastic surgeon had done a masterful job, considering the situation. But anyone could tell that this had been a horrible, horrible wound and a very traumatic experience for the little girl.

Realizing what this whole encounter with the girl had been about, I suddenly became "scar friendly." Thinking it would help the girl feel more comfortable with her scars if she could see mine, I started volunteering scars—showing the girls a scar on my arm from a window accident and another on my ankle from a motorcycle exhaust pipe. The big sister started getting into the act by showing us her scars, too. We were having a "Scar Fest!"

It was then that Dr. Doerring's door opened. A woman

walked out of his office and said, "It's time to go, girls." The girls had been waiting for their mother. I had the right appointment time after all.

I said goodbye to the girls and went into Dr. Doerring's office. He sensed that something significant had happened in the waiting area, and he asked me to tell him about it. I shared with him what had happened, and he found it fascinating that the little girl had asked me about my scar.

But on this day I had come to talk with Dr. Doerring about another kind of scar. Besides the stress of trying to lead two churches and helping Cheri raise four children, I still was having difficulty regarding my stepfather's death. Part of the issue was guilt.

Not long before my stepfather's boating accident, I had planned to come home from New York to Savannah. But just before I was to leave, I got cast in the lead role of a show. If I had come home, there was a good chance that my stepfather would not have gone fishing that fateful Saturday. Also, I was not able to come home for the funeral, because I had a major part in a show that was about to open. I had an understudy, but he had not had time to learn the role. If I had left, it would have put the theatre in a terrible bind.

My family and relatives assured me that they were okay, and they encouraged me to do the show. So I delayed my trip back home, and I missed being with everyone for the funeral and grieving process. I felt so disconnected from the experiences around my stepfather's death.

Dr. Doerring asked me how my stepfather had died. I shared that he and my uncle had gone fishing on a Saturday in September of 1982. The boat struck something solid in the water, throwing both men out of the boat. My uncle survived, but my stepfather did not. "In fact," I said, "it happened in the waters near here—the waters between Bluffton and Hilton Head."

A strange look came over Dr. Doerring's face. "Billy," he said, "I remember it. I remember it well. I was there."

"What do you mean?" I said.

"I happened to be on the dock when they brought your stepfather in. I saw him."

I didn't know quite what to say. It was so strange to have been so far away from the tragic event, and now be connected to someone who had been so close to it. Not even any of my family members had been there when it happened, and yet here I was with a therapist, an agent of healing, who had actually been present. What were the chances that the person I would be led to for healing was actually at the event that I needed healing for—an event that didn't even happen in Savannah?

As I drove back home, I felt good. It was a beautiful day. I had the windows down, letting in the salty, marshy air. I had bonded with a little girl who was willing to share scars. And I felt good because somehow I had ended up with a wonderful therapist, a therapist who in some mysterious way happened to be present at the event I felt so detached from—a therapist who helped in the healing of one of my deepest scars.

THE SONG

In 2001, I got a phone call from a woman named June Joyner, a member of Asbury Memorial. She left a message asking if I would officiate a funeral. I always try to officiate funerals when asked, but this was a particularly rough week for me. I had just gotten back from a long trip to Columbus, Georgia. Not only was I tired from the trip, my family and I were in a middle of a difficult transition.

I had been pastoring two churches for eight years, but that week, I was transitioning to serving only one of the churches. This was going to be an emotional week of moving and saying goodbyes. On top of that, Asbury's theatre was doing something they had never done before—producing one of their musicals during the summer months. Their show, *Children of Eden,* was to open in a week; and I had about 150 errands to run.

I decided that I would call June back and suggest the names of other ministers to officiate the service. It would be best for all involved, as I wouldn't have the time or energy to do an adequate job with the service. But when I returned the call, June informed me that the person who died was her 35-year-old sister. Her sister, Sherry, had been fighting breast cancer and was leaving behind a husband and three young children. This was a funeral I needed to do.

The only time I could meet with the family was the night before the funeral right after the visitation. I got to the funeral home and saw June. She introduced me to her mother and to Sherry's widowed husband. I sat down with the three of them to learn more about Sherry, so I could help them celebrate her life the next morning. But it would be a bittersweet celebration, as Sherry's life was much too short.

"What did Sherry love?" I asked. "What were her passions in life?"

"Her children," said her mother without hesitation. "They were her number one loves in life."

"Dogs and horses," said her sister, June. "Anything that slobbered on her face." After June and her mother offered a few more of Sherry's passions, Sherry's husband spoke up, offering a comment or two. I tried jotting everything down as fast as I could.

I then asked the family if Sherry had a favorite song or hymn that we could play or sing in the service. June and her mother couldn't think of one, but they asked if I would sing something. I told them if I sang a song, it needed to be something the organist at the funeral home was familiar with—we would not have time to rehearse, so the song needed to be something very familiar.

They did not mention any of the funeral standards, like "How Great Thou Art" or "Amazing Grace" or "In the Garden." Nor did I. As wonderful as those songs are, they didn't seem appropriate for the funeral of a 35-year-old woman who was leaving behind a husband and three small children. Surely we could find a song that would be more fitting for this situation—something that would offer them some hope. But what would it be?

I explained to the family that it did not need to be a church song or a hymn, but no one had any ideas. I told them that I would work on it. But I didn't have much time. The funeral was the next day at 10:00 a.m., and I still had to write a eulogy and prepare a service.

I got up early the next morning to work on the eulogy. It was now 9:00, and I still did not have a song. I decided to look quickly through my collection of musical theatre songbooks. I needed to find a song the organist was familiar with, a song the organist and I would not have to rehearse, a song that I was able to sing, and a song that would be meaningful for a husband and three children who had lost their 35-year-old wife and mother.

As I looked at my shelf filled with songbooks, my hand seemed to be drawn to the musical *Carouse*l. Then it came to me. The perfect song would be "You'll Never Walk Alone." It would be familiar for the organist; it was a song we wouldn't have to rehearse; it was a song I could sing; and, most importantly, it was a song that would be meaningful for the family in their difficult situation.

Carousel is about a man named Billy Bigelow, a charming, roguish carnival barker at a carousel. Billy meets a young woman named Julie; they fall in love, get married, and have a child, a daughter. But then Billy dies, leaving them behind. The audience can see Billy after he dies, walking around his wife and daughter as they go through life. Even though they cannot see Billy, he talks to them and encourages them. Many years later, he invisibly attends his daughter's graduation, hoping to help her one last time. He whispers words of encouragement into her ear as everyone sings "You'll Never Walk Alone."

This was the perfect song for Sherry's service. I wanted to convey to her family that Sherry was still alive and that she was still with them, encouraging them, praying for them. I had a strange sensation about this song. It was as though God and Sherry had helped me find it right at the last minute.

As I started to rush out of the house to the funeral home, I decided to look over my notes one last time—the notes I had made the night before at the funeral home. I read over the questions I had asked the family and read their responses.

"What did Sherry love? What were her passions?" Sherry's mother had said, "Her children. They were her number one loves in life." Sister June then added, "Dogs and horses, anything that slobbered on her face." Then Sherry's husband had made a comment or two. I had jotted his thoughts down as fast as I could, but I had not really processed them.

When I read what I had written, I said to myself, "You've got to be kidding." Sherry's husband had said, "Sherry loved to collect carousel horses. She loved carousels."

In the hundreds of funerals that I've done over the years and all the families I've talked to about their loved ones who have died, that's the only time I can recall someone ever mentioning carousels. How often do *you* talk about carousels?

❦

Sherry's mother started attending Asbury Memorial, and it wasn't long before she joined the church. She got very involved in our ministries. Many Asburians now know her as our long-time Hospitality Team coordinator, Chris Beaver.

CANDACE AND BETTY

On a Sunday in October of 2003, I sat in a circle with about 25 people who were planning to join Asbury Memorial United Methodist Church. Three times a year, Asbury offers New Member Classes for people interested in becoming a part of its faith community.

The classes are held on Sundays after the church service for two consecutive weeks. The participants get treated to a fabulous lunch, hosted by Asbury's Hospitality Team. Following the feast, I meet with the group for a time of sharing and information. It also gives people a chance to ask questions about the church.

These classes are very important for me because it's often the first time I get to meet people who are new to Asbury, so I really look forward to this time together. I especially love the first session because I get to hear the participants' stories and learn about their lives. I also love this first session because something incredible usually happens—we all experience wonderful, spiritual moments during this time of sharing.

The main purpose of the first session is to get to know one another. It's a time to start bonding, through the sharing of our stories. We begin by asking each person to respond to the following questions:

What is your name?
Where are you from?
What is your faith background, if you have one?
How did you find Asbury Memorial?

This exercise almost always produces amazing experiences. For instance, when people share their faith background, I'm always fascinated with the amount of diversity in the group. Not only are there people who grew up in traditional Protestant denominations—Baptist, Presbyterian, Lutheran, Episcopal, or United Methodist—there usually are people who grew up Roman Catholic and Pentecostal. And there usually are others who did not have any religious experience at all.

When people take their turn, some tell of their positive experiences with religion while others share painful memories of it. It's amazing how the people connect with one another through this sharing. Somehow, this world that is so big and diverse becomes small and family-like as we share our common experiences and feelings.

Although I know that most of the participants will feel comfortable after they experience this first session of sharing, I often am concerned about them before the session as they eat together for the first time. Here are people who are new to the church—people who don't know one another—and they are stepping into the unknown process of joining a church. Most of us don't like the unknown, so I know this experience must raise their anxiety level a bit. So I find myself concerned about them. I always look forward to seeing these "strangers" relax and bond with one another during the first session.

❦

As I sat in a circle with the class in October of 2003, I was wondering how everyone was doing—how they were feeling—what they were thinking.

One of the persons in the class was a young mother named Candace Jenkins. Candace had not been attending Asbury very long, so she did not know many people at the church. She especially didn't know the people in the class. They were all new to her.

Sitting next to her was an older woman named Betty Hohnerlein. Like Candace, Betty had been attending Asbury only for a short time. She, too, didn't know many people. So here were these two women—in this new surrounding—with new people—willing to take this big step.

We went around the circle and introduced ourselves. When it was Betty's turn, she said, "My name is Betty Hohnerlein."

Before she could say another word, Candace gasped and said, "Mrs. Hohnerlein, are you John's mother?"

Betty said, "Yes."

Candace reached out and hugged Betty and said, "I knew you looked familiar! I knew you looked familiar!" Then Candace turned to the rest of us and proclaimed, "I knew she looked familiar! I knew she looked familiar!"

We all laughed, but had no idea what was going on.

Candace turned back to Betty and said, "Betty, my maiden name is Carlyle. I am Candace Carlyle, Rob's sister." Betty let out a gasp and hugged Candace with great fervor.

Then, Candace let the rest of us know what was going on. She told us that she had a brother named Rob, who, unfortunately had died at a young age. She had been very close to Rob, for, you see, Rob not only was her brother, he was her twin. She obviously loved her twin brother, and when Candace gave birth to a baby boy, she named him "Robbie," after her brother. She went on to tell the group that Betty has a son whose name is John. John had been her brother Rob's best friend.

Candace later told me the rest of the story. Rob and John became friends near the end of high school. They became close during their years in college, and both moved to Atlanta after graduating. They eventually bought a house together and remained close for many years until Rob's death in 1995 at the age of 29.

Candace said that Rob hadn't been very open with his family about how sick he was. She later found out that John had been there every day for Rob—saw his illness and took wonderful care of him. The last time Candace went to Atlanta to see Rob before he moved back to Savannah, when he knew he was dying, she saw how sick he was becoming. She also witnessed John being there for him and helping him in every way. She said that John dealt with the medicines and all that came with the sickness as only a loving soul could do.

When Rob decided to move back to Savannah, he told Candace how sad he was about leaving John and how he would be forever grateful for the way John had taken care of him. He said nobody should have to endure seeing someone that sick and step in and handle it the way John did.

Rob moved back to Savannah and died four weeks later.

Candace adored her brother, and she is forever grateful for John and his compassionate presence in her brother's life.

So eight years later, two strangers are sitting next to each other in a social hall of an inner city church as part of a New Member Class—two strangers who were not really strangers, two people who were joined at the hip more than they could ever imagine. To this day, Candace and Betty look for each other on Sundays and sit together at church.

By the way, Betty's son, John, has since joined the church too. He lives in Charleston, South Carolina, but he often makes the two-hour trip to Asbury Memorial in order to worship God, to see his mother, and to see his best friend's twin sister.

Mary and Wiley

One of the most famous stories of synchronicity involved the deaths of John Adams and Thomas Jefferson, the two main architects of the Declaration of Independence and the American Revolution. The second and third presidents of the United States were close friends, then bitter rivals, and then friends again. They were the last surviving members of the original American revolutionaries. During their later years, they often wrote letters to each other.

Ironically, Adams and Jefferson both died of natural causes on the same day at their homes—Adams in Massachusetts and Jefferson in Virginia. Even more incredible, they died on July 4, 1826, the 50th anniversary of the adoption of the Declaration of Independence. If that's not a wow moment, I don't know what is!

Asbury Memorial has its own Adams and Jefferson story. In fact, it involves another Adams, Mary Adams. She was one of the great matriarchs of Asbury Memorial United Methodist Church. Before I met Mary, I had heard about her from the other elderly members of the church. You could tell that they revered Mary Adams.

When I met Mary, it didn't take long for me to fall in love with her too. You enjoyed being in her presence. Although she was elderly, she was spirited and frisky. She almost seemed like a teenager—full of life, love, and personality. She loved to laugh and poke fun at herself, saying things like, "When I die, Billy, make sure my wig is on straight in the casket!"

She was also prone to calling people "rascals." Being a rascal in Mary's book was a good thing. You were a rascal if you liked to be adventurous and have fun.

Mary and I had a special connection. She loved Norman Vincent Peale. She loved the fact that I used to be at his church in New York. Mary and her husband, Lamar, met Dr. Peale many years ago in Savannah. They had picked him up at the airport when he came to speak to a bunch of Methodists in South Georgia.

By the time I started at Asbury Memorial, Lamar had already died. Mary was a widow, living by herself at home. She and Lamar did not have children. The members of Asbury Memorial were her family. Mary had been active in about every group and organization at the church. When she reached her late 80s, she could not attend Sunday services as frequently—a bad case of vertigo was one of the culprits. After she reached her 90s, she stayed at home and worshiped with us in spirit.

One of Mary's best friends was Wiley Kessler. Wiley was even older than Mary. He had been just as involved at the church as Mary. Wiley had been a bass soloist in the choir, served as a Sunday School teacher, helped lead the youth, and held a variety of positions on many church committees. He had the same kind of sense of humor and fun personality as Mary.

Wiley's wife was named Myra. Not long after I started working at Asbury, Myra became ill and had to move into a nursing home. For years, until the day she died, Wiley would travel to the nursing home every day to be with Myra. After her death, Wiley had a bad fall at his home and had to move into the very same facility.

He didn't seem to mind too much. He already knew the staff and other residents because of all the time he had spent with Myra there. Every time I went to visit him, he was spry and spirited. Though he was 101, Wiley was in great shape. Folks often told the joke that Wiley took less medication than either of his sons. But it wasn't a joke—it was true. Wiley was in remarkable condition.

When Mary and Wiley were younger, they both worked with the youth of the church. You can imagine what it was like for the youth to be led by these two spirited and spunky individuals. The youth must have loved them! Stories are still circulating about the good times the young people had with Mary and Wiley.

The widow and widower had served the church for so many years together. They had seen the church at its prime during the 1940s, 1950s, and 1960s, had seen it decline in the 1970s and 1980s, and had watched it almost close in the early 1990s. Fortunately, they both were able to see the revitalization of the church in the mid-1990s.

Through the years of knowing each other and serving together, Mary and Wiley became soul mates. They talked on the phone at least twice a day, sometimes more. When you thought of Mary, you thought of Wiley. When you thought of Wiley, you thought of Mary.

❦

On the morning of Saturday, December 4, 2004, I got a phone call from Mary's niece. She wanted to let me know that Mary had died that morning in her sleep. She had not been sick, but she was 96 years old. She had died at home of natural causes.

What about Wiley? I was afraid someone would call him and tell him about Mary's death over the phone and no one would be there to comfort him. I rushed to the nursing home. That way, I could tell Wiley in person and be with him.

When I arrived, I was surprised to find Wiley hunched over in his wheelchair. He was hardly able to move or communicate. This was highly unusual. In spite of his age, Wiley was always upbeat and feisty. I was so concerned about his demeanor that I asked the nursing staff to call Wiley's sons so they could come check on him.

As I knelt beside his wheelchair holding his hand, I started to tell Wiley about Mary. When I mentioned her name, he squeezed my hand. I believe he wanted to know how his old friend was doing. I then shared with him that Mary had passed away that morning. Wiley let out a soft groan. I then offered a prayer.

I didn't want to leave Wiley, but I needed to go be with Mary's family at the funeral home so we could plan her funeral service. I informed the nursing staff that Wiley had just lost a close friend and asked if they would keep a special watch on him.

Off I went to meet with Mary's family and the funeral

director, Hubert Baker. Many years before, Hubert had been the church organist at Asbury Memorial. He knew all of the older members at the church. He was especially close to Mary, and he would take great care in helping with her funeral arrangements.

When I arrived at the funeral home, I went to a back room where ministers meet with the family of the deceased. Sitting around a large table was Mary's niece, Paula, and Paula's husband, Chuck. Hubert had not yet arrived. I shared with Paula and Chuck that I had come from seeing Wiley at the nursing home and that I had told him about Mary's death.

Just as we were about to start talking about Mary's service, one of the funeral directors came into the room. He said that there was an important phone call for me and that I could take it in Hubert's office. I went to the office and picked up the phone.

"Billy," the voice said, "this is Hubert. Wiley Kessler just died. Can you believe it?"

I couldn't believe it. Yet, it seemed appropriate for these two great soul mates to make their transition together.

I went back to the room where Paula and Chuck were sitting and shared with them the news. They, too, were in disbelief.

Best friends and soul mates—one living 96 years on this earth and the other living 101 years, dying of natural causes within hours of each other—go figure.

Paula said, "There's no doubt that Aunt Mary was coaxing Wiley to join her. I'm sure she was there to welcome him home."

Mary…You rascal!

Jekyll and Hyde

In October of 2005, I got a call from a young mother at our church named Kim. She was calling to see if I could baptize her two young children. Kim and her husband, Mark, had a three-year-old boy named Hank and a one-year-old girl named Olivia. Kim knew it was short notice, but she was wondering if I could baptize Hank and Olivia on Sunday, October 30th.

I normally do all I can to accommodate parents and their children's baptisms. But as I looked at the calendar, I saw a problem. During the month of October, we offer very unique and creative worship services. These services are developed around particular books, movies, or theatrical themes. We have found that the themes of these stories can enhance the worship experience—whether it's the prayers, the music, the sermons, or the liturgies.

When we have these creative services and someone asks for baptism, I will weave the baptism into the service. But October 30, 2005, was definitely not a good day for the baptisms of two young children. Why? Because the theme we were using that Sunday was based on the classic story of Dr. Jekyll and Mr. Hyde. The music would be darker than normal. Even the sanctuary itself would be darker. The choir would be dressed in black. This was not the Sunday for the joyful baptisms of two young children.

"Kim," I said, "is it possible for you to choose another Sunday?"

"I'm wanting that particular date because my parents will be visiting from Pennsylvania," she replied.

"Kim, let me explain to you the situation." I told her why I had my reservations. I told her about the theme of the service and that I really thought they would have a better experience if they chose a different Sunday.

"But Billy, I have no idea when my parents will be in Savannah again," she said.

"Okay," I said, "We'll work it into the service somehow."

I hung up the phone wondering what in the world I was going to do. We usually have baptisms during the first part of a worship service. That way, if children get antsy during the service, the parents can take them out of the sanctuary. But there was no way we could have Hank and Olivia's baptisms at the beginning of the Jekyll and Hyde Service. Everything would be dark, almost scary. Since the movement of the service would be going from dark to light, the baptisms would have to be near the end.

Our Worship Team had worked hard at designing a meaningful service for that Sunday. Sometimes we like to have some levity in the service, and we created it by having the announcements done by two people, one being Dr. Henry Jekyll and the other being Edward Hyde. After the announcements, we moved back into the seriousness of the service.

The hymns, the sermon, and our liturgies were very

powerful, as they focused on our identities and those parts of ourselves we keep hidden. We then spoke of the redemptive and transforming power of God. We had moved from the darkness into the light, and now it was time for the baptisms.

Mark and Kim came forward, holding their two beautiful blonde children in their arms. The children were dressed all in white. Their baptisms would be the perfect ending, reminding us that God leads us out of darkness into light. The baptisms would also be perfect reminders that God loves us just as we are—warts and all. This was a great Sunday to baptize these two children after all.

As the parents stood in front of me—each of them holding a child, I prepared to baptize Hank first. To make sure I said his correct first and middle names, I looked down at the names in the bulletin. As I prepared to pronounce Hank's full name for baptism, I did a double take. I couldn't believe what I was seeing.

Whenever a child is baptized in one of our services, we always list his or her full name in the bulletin. Hank's name was "Henry Edward." Henry Edward…Henry Edward. Those were the very names of Jekyll and Hyde. The entire service and my entire sermon had revolved around "Henry" Jekyll and "Edward" Hyde.

When I pointed out this incredible coincidence to the congregation, there was a mixture of "oohs" and "ahs"—and some chuckles. What got us chuckling even more was the fact that little Hank received his baptism very graciously and quietly. When it came time for little sister Olivia to be baptized, she started screaming at the top of her lungs, right on cue! She screamed and screamed! I, of course, was sorry that little Olivia was so upset, but it was perfect! She was perfect! The baptisms of these two children physically and emotionally demonstrated the story of Jekyll and Hyde, and the grace that's offered to all of us!

Sometime later, as I thought more about this meaningful coincidence, I started wondering about Olivia's full name and what it might mean. So I did some research.

I discovered that Olivia means "Olive Tree" which, of course, has become a symbol for peace. And Olivia's middle name? "Kristof." Olivia Kristof. Kristof means, "Bearer of Christ." I should have known.

For in these two children, who were baptized on "Jekyll and Hyde Sunday," were the perfect examples of what we were trying to communicate and experience on that particular Sunday. The baptism that I thought would be a problem ended up being a great blessing. It was almost as if it was ordained by God, the One who loves and cares for both Jekylls and Hydes.

BOBBY

Soon after I starting pastoring at Asbury Memorial in 1993, a congregation of another church asked if they could use our sanctuary for a special event. They were hosting an out of town speaker who might appeal to many people in the Savannah area. Their sanctuary, however, was small and could only seat 100 people. Even though we had a small congregation, our sanctuary was large and could hold 500.

The speaker was a man who had a fascinating story. While he was talking on the telephone during a thunderstorm, he was struck by lightning. He appeared to be dead for almost half an hour. But after being unconscious, he revived. He's been telling his story ever since.

Even though our church wasn't sponsoring the event, I was interested in hearing the man's fascinating story. Plus, someone had to turn off the lights and lock up the building. That night, the man shared with the audience what he experienced while he had been deceased. He made a statement I will never forget, "If you only remember one thing that I share with you tonight, remember this: You are as dead now as you will ever be."

I have shared that statement at numerous funerals I have officiated. I have also shared statements by Dr. Elizabeth

Kübler-Ross, who basically said the same thing. Dr. Kübler-Ross was the Swiss psychiatrist who spent thousands of hours observing people who were dying. She perhaps studied the dying and death experience more than any human being.

When she began her studies, she was an atheist. She changed her mind, however, after being with so many people as they made their transition. She said that it became obvious from her experiences with people who were dying that life is transcendent. She also came to believe that loved ones who had already passed to the other side would be there to help and greet us when we made our transition.

The afterlife is a mystery, of course. We all want to know more about it. We have heard or read stories of near-death experiences. Some of them seem fabricated while others do not. We would love for someone to solve this great mystery for us.

If you are curious about the subject, I encourage you to read the book *Life Begins at Death* by the English clergyman and theologian, Leslie Weatherhead. I highly recommend it.

In 2005, an old family friend named Marvin Grimm died at the age of 87. I was asked to officiate Mr. Grimm's funeral service. I had known him my entire life. He was an active member of the church I attended as a child and youth. He was a good man, who had led a good life.

As I prepared Mr. Grimm's eulogy for the funeral, I felt led to share the story of the man who had come to speak at Asbury—the man who had died and said, "You're as dead now as you will ever be." I also felt led to share some writings of Elizabeth Kübler-Ross—about her belief that dying is like being born, born into another existence—and her belief that we have loved ones on the other side, helping us make our transition.

I felt very strongly about sharing these remarks, but I also was somewhat hesitant. Mr. Grimm and his family had been part of the church for many years. They were used to more traditional language about death and resurrection. I thought my remarks may sound a little too untraditional for them. Since I didn't want to make the Grimm family uncomfortable during the service, I decided to refrain from sharing these additional remarks and to stick to the more traditional Christian language.

So that's what I did and that's what I said—and that's when it happened. For some reason after I finished my "traditional" remarks, I felt compelled to share my other thoughts, hoping the Grimms would find them comforting and not awkward. I then said a prayer and a closing benediction.

Immediately after the service, one of Mr. Grimm's daughters, Mina Smith, came up to me. She seemed eager to talk. "Billy," she said, "I'm so glad you said what you did today. Did you hear what happened to Bobby?"

Bobby was her nephew. He was a special child in the family. Bobby was born with severe disabilities—mentally and physically. He had difficulty walking and talking. Bobby was loved and cherished by his family and by his church family. Because of all of the love that surrounded him and because of Bobby's own determination, he did remarkably well for someone with all of his challenges. He grew into a fine young man and even started helping his father and mother at the store they owned in Savannah. Unfortunately, Bobby's mother became ill and died in 1999. A number of years later, his father remarried.

When Mina came up to me and asked me if I had heard what happened to Bobby, I said, "No. What happened?"

"A couple of weeks ago," Mina said," Bobby was eating supper with his family. All of a sudden, he choked on his food. He couldn't breathe. He started turning blue, and he went unconscious. They thought they had lost him. Eventually, they were able to bring him back and got him to breathe. But they couldn't believe what he told them. When he was able to speak, he said, 'I saw momma. I saw momma. She told me to go back and live with daddy and his new wife.'"

I appreciate the words of the man who came to speak at Asbury Memorial. I appreciate the words of the great psychiatrist, Elizabeth Kübler-Ross. As much as I believe and appreciate their words, I believe and appreciate Bobby's even more.

Here was a young man who was as innocent as a dove—who had no preconceived notions—who wouldn't even know what the word "fabricate" means. Bobby's words came from a heart that only knew how to share what he had experienced openly and honestly.

When I officiate funerals, I still sometimes quote the man who came and shared at the church, and I still sometimes quote Dr. Elizabeth Kübler-Ross. But when I think of after-death experiences, the first person I think of is Bobby Smith.

A little over a month after Mr. Grimm's funeral, Bobby died again. This time he stayed with his mother.

Rest in peace, Bobby. We will see you again someday.

THE CLOCK

When I came to Asbury Memorial in June of 1993, the chancel choir consisted of four people, four older women. Two of the four were Jane Corbin and Virginia Holliday. Jane and Virginia had been in the choir for many years. Jane had been one of the choir's soloists during Asbury's glory days in the 1960s. After Asbury's revitalization in the 1990s, the church grew and so did the choir. By 2008, the choir had 40 to 50 members; among them were the two good friends, Jane and Virginia.

Jane picked Virginia up every Wednesday night to go to choir practice. Virginia, 84 years old at the time, did not drive, but not because of her age. She had never driven—never owned a car. If Virginia went somewhere, she walked, took a bus, or got a lift from a friend. She was in the best shape of any 84-year-old you've ever met. And she's currently in the best shape of any 92-year-old you'll ever meet.

Everyone at the church is amazed at Virginia. We have never seen someone her age so active. Of course, one of the reasons she is in good shape is because she walks so much. Her health is supported by her daily habits and routine. Every day Virginia gets up very early in the morning and rakes her front lawn. Granted, her front lawn is very small and doesn't consist of much grass. But if you go by Virginia's house each morning, you always see fresh rake lines in the dirt.

During her career years, Virginia worked at Memorial Hospital doing custodial work. She would catch a bus every day at 5:30 a.m. to go work at the hospital. Virginia worked there for 24 years and *never* missed a day of work. She's probably the only employee in the history of Memorial who can say that. She is the most consistent person I've ever seen. Her good friend Jane would often say, "Virginia is always there. She is like clockwork—just like clockwork."

When the church started having Wednesday Night Suppers, Jane picked Virginia up to get to the church early so they could get things ready. They focused on decorating the tables, putting out the placemats, and doing the table settings. Virginia was known for getting all of the drinks ready; in fact, Virginia still prepares the tea, lemonade, coffee, and water for all of the church functions. After supper, Jane and Virginia went to choir practice; then Jane took Virginia home, just a few blocks away from the church.

In 2008, Jane was diagnosed with cancer. Eventually she was taken to Hospice House where she would spend her last days. One of the most powerful and moving moments I've ever experienced was when 40-plus members of the choir went to Hospice House, stood outside the sliding glass door leading to Jane's room, and serenaded the long-time choir member and soloist with beautiful music. I get goose bumps recalling that moment. Of course, many of us were concerned about Virginia and how she was handling Jane's illness and anticipated death.

❦

On Wednesday night, October 29th, the phone rang about 11:00. It was Jane's daughter, Janie. She was calling to let me know that Jane had just died. She said that the family had been with her, and had just left for the night. Many people who are dying wait until their family and friends are gone before they pass. Some people want to be alone when they make the transition, while others want family members with them. Jane apparently had wanted to be alone. Soon after the family left, Jane let go and died. The staff estimated the time of her death as around 10:30 p.m.

When Janie called me, she said, "Mom is out of pain now. My biggest concern is Virginia. This is going to be so hard for her." Janie and I decided that since it was so late at night, we wouldn't wake Virginia up and tell her the sad news, especially since she lived by herself. Janie said that she would call Virginia and tell her around six in the morning. We both knew that Virginia would have already been up for almost two hours by then. I told Janie that I would go by and spend time with Virginia in the morning and see how she was doing.

❦

So that's what happened. Janie called Virginia and told her the news. I went over a little later to be with her. As I was sitting with Virginia in her living room, I mentioned that it was special that Jane made her transition on a Wednesday night, the night that had always been so special for the two of them—with Wednesday Night Supper and choir practice.

Then Virginia stood up and said, "Follow me. I want to show you something." She led me into the next room and pointed to the mantle.

"What is it, Virginia?"

She said, "Look at the clock on the mantle." On the mantle was a beautiful antique clock.

Still not understanding her, I said, "What about the clock?"

She said, "Look what time it is." I looked at the clock and it read 10:24. "The clock stopped at 10:24 last night," she said. Then I realized what Virginia was getting at—Jane had died alone; and the estimated time of her death was 10:30. Virginia believed she knew exactly when Jane made her transition. She believed the clock stopped for a reason.

I thought it was an interesting coincidence, but Cheri and I have an old wind-up clock that frequently stops. Just to be curious, I said, "Virginia, when's the last time that clock stopped?"

She said, "It's never stopped—never stopped that I know of. I wind it twice a week. I guess it could have stopped when my mother was alive over 11 years ago, but it's never stopped that I know of."

I believe an old friend was letting her old friend know that she was okay. One thing is for sure. The clock didn't stop because Virginia forgot to wind it. We know that's not the case—because as Jane used to say: "Virginia is always there. She is like clockwork—just like clockwork."

Kit and Ken

On Friday, April 9, 2009, I sat quietly in a movie theatre enjoying a film while a number of people were frantically trying to reach me by phone. Not only did I not have my cell phone with me, I didn't know where it was. I had misplaced it.

Later that night, I found the phone. I had four messages on it. The first message was from a local wedding coordinator. He said, "Rev. Hester, just kind of wondering where you are. Hopefully you're nearby. We're just getting a little nervous."

Apparently I was supposed to have officiated a wedding that afternoon. The other three messages were also from the wedding coordinator. I can't tell you what he said in those messages!

This is a minister's worst nightmare! I have been in ministry for 27 years and have done over two hundred weddings. Never before had I forgotten a wedding I was supposed to officiate. This was my first and, hopefully, my last.

❦

I actually was supposed to do two weddings that Friday. But about a week before the services, the wedding coordinator called to tell me that an old friend of one of the couples was a minister and had decided to officiate their ceremony himself. I took a pencil and scratched through that wedding on my calendar. In doing so, I obstructed my view of the other wedding. I knew I had another wedding that weekend, and I saw some things listed on my calendar for Saturday. I assumed that the second wedding was on Saturday.

When I discovered what had happened late Friday night around 10:00, I couldn't get in touch with anyone. The couple was from out of town. I had never met them, and I didn't have their phone number. I called the wedding coordinator, only to get his answering machine. He probably wouldn't have wanted to talk to me anyway. I sent him an email offering my deepest apologies and tried to explain what happened. I didn't mention that I was enjoying a movie while he was going through this terrible ordeal.

I wondered what had happened to the bride and groom. Did they get married? Was the wedding coordinator able to find another minister? Did I need to run downtown to perform a midnight ceremony? Were they able to have a reception? Or did they have to tell everyone to go home? That would have been difficult since everyone was from out of town.

Welcome to Savannah!

Late that night, I finally got an email from the wedding coordinator. He said that they finally had found a minister, and that the couple did get married. But of course, they had experienced a great deal of stress and anxiety.

I couldn't believe what I had done. I couldn't get to sleep

at all that night. I tossed and turned, tossed and turned—I had to get up and watch television in order to try to forget about it. All I could think about was the bride wanting this to be such a special day—her dream day—and I had ruined it for her and the groom.

I tried to use it as a teaching moment for my young sons—trying to squeeze out some bit of redemption. "Boys, dad made a really bad mistake. I didn't look carefully at my calendar, and I messed things up for some people. See how important it is to look at your assignments. Learn from my mistake."

Saturday I felt much the same way—I couldn't get my big blunder off my mind. The very next day was Palm Sunday, one of the biggest days in the Christian year. I had a lot to prepare for. I had to get ready for the Palm Sunday service and the start of Holy Week, the busiest time of the year for the church. But I couldn't concentrate. I couldn't sit still at my desk. I had to be moving. I decided to do manual work at the church. I worked all day moving things—going upstairs and downstairs, upstairs and downstairs, upstairs and downstairs. It was as though I was doing penance.

I finally became physically exhausted. Then I had to go home to work on a Palm Sunday sermon. Fortunately, I have always loved the natural theme of religion and politics for Palm Sunday, so I was able to put a sermon together. But I was still feeling the weight and guilt of what I had done.

❦

We ended up having a wonderful Palm Sunday service. As the choir was singing the benediction, I walked down the center aisle to get ready to greet people on their way out of the sanctuary. Since it was Palm Sunday, there were more people than usual—more hugs and handshakes than most Sundays.

As the crowd began to thin out, I noticed a man and woman who seemed to be waiting at the very end of the line. I could tell they were lingering, as if they wanted to wait till everyone had left so they could talk with me. No, they were not the couple I was to marry the day before. This couple looked familiar to me, but I couldn't place them. I knew they weren't regular attenders.

The line finally whittled down to the end, leaving only the couple standing in front of me. "Do you remember us?" they said. Whenever someone asks me that question my first inclination is to think they are someone Cheri and I knew from our days in New York—people who are in town visiting Savannah.

I said, "I know that I know you. I just can't place you. You look so familiar."

The man said, "We're Ken and Kit. You married us almost one year ago today. We live in Duluth, Georgia. We came to Savannah last year and you were kind enough to marry us. We thought for our first-year anniversary we would come back to Savannah. We remembered you telling us about your church, so we wanted to come see you. We loved the service. We wish we lived closer so we could come every week."

I looked at this couple and said, "You don't know how good it is to see you and what your visit means to me today."

❦

Kit and Ken had no idea what had happened that weekend. They didn't know that I had been beating myself up for two days and felt like a heel about the wedding I had messed up. These two out-of-towners picked just the right Sunday to visit Savannah and come to the church. They lifted my spirits!

Although I had made a bad mistake that weekend, Kit and Ken helped me realize that I had also been part of something good. Two people from out of town—two people who came to Savannah to get married—helped me heal from hurting two other people who came to Savannah to get married. This moment of grace helped me to embrace the part of me that messes up and makes mistakes. I was able to let go and start living again.

Although Easter was the following Sunday, I had already experienced a resurrection. Thanks to Kit and Ken, Easter came early for me. They helped me experience new life, a new perspective, and the grace of God.

The Pipe Organ

James Garvin and I grew up at Epworth United Methodist Church in Savannah. James was four years older than me, so we were not in the same Sunday School classes or youth group. He was closer to my sister's age. But I also knew James through his mother and his younger sister, Carmel. His mother, Mary Alice Garvin, was one of my first choir directors. The Hester and Garvin families have had a close relationship for many years.

James was an incredible musician. He was the drum major for the Savannah High School Marching Band, which was a great honor. In those days, Savannah High always had one of the top bands in the state. Standing over six feet tall—a long, tall hat on his head and a baton in his gloved hand—James made a striking figure as drum major. Conducting with great precision and control, James was in his element.

Another outstanding musician in Savannah at that time was Sumner Thorpe. She *ruled* the organ at Epworth UMC, and was Savannah's own "Phantom of the Opera." One Sunday, I saw James sitting behind Miss Thorpe's organ. I didn't think anyone was allowed to be at the keys of her organ. But there was James, sitting up there on the bench all by himself, as if he belonged.

James went on to become an organ expert. He left

Savannah to study and train in London. He worked on pipe organs in famous cathedrals and churches in Europe. He became widely known for his expertise in the rebuilding, repairing, and tuning of pipe organs.

He got his love for the instrument naturally. His mother and father were passionate musicians, and both played the piano and organ. Legend has it that Ed and Mary Alice Garvin courted each other on a piano bench.

Ed is deceased now; but Mary Alice, now in her mid-eighties, still plays the organ for church and funeral services. One of the great benefits of moving back to Savannah was reconnecting with Mary Alice and getting to work with her. She and I have done over a hundred funerals together and continue to do so.

I had lost touch with James over the years. He married and moved to Jacksonville, Florida. In November of 2010, I got a phone call from his sister, Carmel, telling me that James had died of cancer at the age of 55. She asked me to help officiate his service, which was to be at his church in Jacksonville on Tuesday, November 16.

As I finished writing the eulogy on Tuesday morning and was trying to get on the road for the two-hour drive to Jacksonville, I checked my email. One of the emails was from an Asbury member named Howard Hackney. Howard wrote, "I saw this today and wanted to share it with you, Billy. Enjoy!" There was an attachment. But whatever Howard wanted me to enjoy would have to wait, because I needed to get on the road to Florida.

When I arrived in Jacksonville and walked into the

church, the first thing I noticed was the large pipe organ. I guess I shouldn't have been surprised. It would only make sense for James to be attending a church that had a beautiful pipe organ.

I learned that the church had burned down a few years earlier. This new sanctuary was built with the design of having the pipe organ as the central feature. And, of course, James designed it! He also oversaw the building of this new 60-rank Schlueter Pipe Organ.

I don't believe I've ever been part of a funeral service where there was such a prominent visual reminder of the deceased and his talents. There in front of us were the great pipes that James had designed and maintained. When we sang the hymns and heard the glorious music coming from the pipes, one couldn't help but think of James and his passion for music and pipe organs.

It was odd seeing his mother, Mary Alice, sitting on one of the front rows during a funeral. She was usually sitting at the organ, helping to lead the service. But this, of course, was the service for her child—her son—something no parent should have to experience. I so wished there was some way to comfort her.

It was a very meaningful and uplifting service. The loft was filled with members of the choir. It was impressive to see that so many of the choir members attended the service, especially since the service was held on a weekday, when people would need to get off from work. It was obvious that they wanted to be there to celebrate the life of a friend and to honor someone who had contributed greatly to the church's music ministry.

When he discovered that he was dying, James wanted to be involved in his funeral service. He selected all of the music—the hymns, the anthem, and a beautiful song of praise that the choir sang at the close of the service. This last song sounded magnificent with the glorious sounds of the pipe organ and the strong voices of the choir. James knew how he wanted to end his service. He left us leaving the sanctuary soaring high with this great song of strength, faith, and hope.

Unlike many services when the burial directly follows the funeral, this interment would be different. James' body was to be brought back to Savannah for burial in a family plot. We were to meet at the cemetery the following day on Wednesday.

That next morning, the day of the interment, I checked my email again. Among them was an email from church member Sam Durham. Sam had written, "When you need a make-me-feel-good experience, check this out." Well, after doing James' funeral the day before, I needed a feel-good experience.

I was about to open the attachment when I noticed that it had the same web address as the email Howard Hackney had sent me the day before. Both Howard and Sam *really* wanted me to see something.

❦

When I opened the attachment, I watched a YouTube presentation that stunned me. It had occurred three weeks earlier on October 30th at the Macy's Department Store in Philadelphia, which is no ordinary department store. It is in a huge, historic building called the Wanamaker Building. Do you know what the Wanamaker is famous for? Built in 1910, it houses the world's largest pipe organ!

The Macy's store features a ten-story marble atrium at its center. A layer-cake of balconies surrounds three sides of the atrium. The fourth side houses the world's largest pipe organ—all 28,400 pipes!

At noon on October 30th, the largest pipe organ in the world started playing Handel's *Hallelujah Chorus*. It sounded as though all the stops were pulled out as the glorious music wafted up the ten-floor atrium. Hundreds of shoppers slowed down or halted their pace and started listening.

What they did not know was that six hundred of the shoppers were actually recruits of the Opera Company of Philadelphia. They had strategically planned with the organist to sing the *Hallelujah Chorus* at twelve noon. As you might guess, when it came time to sing the words of the *Hallelujah Chorus,* the singing shoppers let it rip! The sound of 600-plus voices with the largest pipe organ in the world was divine! That's what Howard and Sam wanted me to experience.

But unknown to Howard and Sam, I was experiencing something even more divine. Because the day before I had officiated the funeral for a man who had dedicated his life to pipe organs, and I was just about to do the interment service for the man who had dedicated his life to pipe organs. Howard and Sam did not know James and had no idea that I was in the throes of doing the services of "Mr. Pipe Organ."

Do you know how long it's been since someone has sent me an email about a pipe organ? That's a silly question, because I've never, ever received an email about a pipe organ! And no one has sent me one since!

If you had told me that I would be receiving an email with a YouTube presentation featuring the largest pipe organ in the world on the day of James' funeral, I would have thought you were crazy. If you had told me I would be receiving the same email from someone else on the day of James' burial, I would have *known* you were crazy!

Since I opened Sam and Howard's email before I went to the burial, I had the opportunity to share what had happened with Mary Alice and those gathered at the cemetery. For me, this strange coincidence was a way of offering us comfort—a reminder that there is a Higher Power who is there for us—and a reminder that James is alive and well in all of God's glory.

One last thing—here comes the crescendo!

Do you remember that the choir ended James' service with a glorious song of praise—a song James had selected and wanted for the end of his service? Believe it or not, James had chosen Handel's *Hallelujah Chorus*—the very same song that the great organ and choir had performed at the Wanamaker. Wow!

For the Lord God omnipotent reigneth!
Hallelujah!

THE FOOTBALL COACH

The first time I met John Carlton "Jug" Knight was in 1966 when I was six years old. He was the head coach of my football team, the Bacon Park Eagles. Coach Knight not only looked the part, he sounded like it. He had a guttural, raspy voice that would make a drill sergeant envious. In spite of his intimidating pipes, his words were always encouraging to his players. He loved young people.

After his sons got older and graduated to another level of football, Coach Knight handed the Eagles team over to two other fine coaches, Donald West and L.A. Lanier. Coaches West and Lanier developed the Eagles into a team that won the city championship year after year after year.

Though Coach Knight and I rarely saw each other after those early years of football, I would see his wife, Claire, on occasion. She owned a bridal shop in Savannah called The Hitching Post. Since I officiated many weddings, and since Claire was known in town as a "wedding expert," our paths would often cross.

Claire had been a fine athlete in her own right. When she was in high school, she helped form a new basketball team for women in Savannah—which led to the forming of a new men's basketball team—which led to her meeting Jug. The boys' team consisted of young men who served in World War

II and returned home. One of those young men—the one who "looked older than the rest," as Claire would say—was Jug. He and Claire dated and were soon married, a marriage that lasted 65 years.

A handful of years ago, I went up to the front of the sanctuary to lead the worship service at Asbury Memorial, and I saw Jug and Claire sitting among the congregation. It was easy to spot Claire, as she is always smartly-dressed and wears wonderful hats. I was surprised to see them because the Knights had been long-time members of another church in Savannah. After the service, I didn't question why they were there—just rejoiced in seeing them again.

Everyone quickly learned that Jug was one of my first football coaches. Many of our church members already knew Claire from her wedding business. The Knights started attending Asbury periodically; and, before long, they started coming regularly. I surprised them one Sunday by bringing to church the 1966 picture of the old football team. Everyone enjoyed seeing the "younger" Jug and the "little" Billy.

During these later years with my old coach, I learned a lot about John Carlton Knight. Jug, as many of his friends called him, served under General Patton in World War II. The War took him to France, Germany, Luxembourg, and the Battle of the Bulge.

I also discovered that my old football coach was a great cook—specializing in pound cake and homemade eggnog—which I got to sample every Christmas. You have not had eggnog until you have had "Jug Knight Eggnog!" Every Christmas, I made sure that he didn't forget to bring me some after he made his annual batch.

I also discovered that Jug was a long-time Mason and that, after he retired, he spent much of his time with fellow Shriners, raising funds to benefit children in need of medical services. That wasn't too much of a surprise, as Jug always was doing something to help young people.

The biggest surprise was discovering that Jug Knight was a top-notch dancer. Jug and Claire loved to dance. How wonderful it was to see them at our church dances. He was the real deal on the dance floor. When I went to see Jug in the hospital after he had knee replacement surgery, he said that he needed to get back on his feet soon so he could go to the next church dance. Not bad for a man in his late 80s.

After getting to reconnect with my old coach and having him as part of my congregation for several years, Jug's health began to decline. On July 9, 2014, at the age of 90, Jug Knight died and made his transition.

We had a wonderful service for Jug and his family and friends. We had Big Band music from the 1940s playing as people entered the sanctuary, and "The Caissons Go Rolling Along" playing as they left. In between, we sang beautiful hymns of faith and songs of patriotism. It was a good send-off for John Carlton Knight, my old football coach.

Six months later, Asbury Memorial was having one of its New Member Classes for people interested in joining the church. There would be two sessions at the end of January, with the class joining on February 1, 2015.

When I saw the list of names of people who had signed up for the class, I was surprised to see Claire's name. Claire and Jug had been coming to Asbury for a long time. They didn't have to join the church "officially" to be part of our faith community. They were already a part of the church family.

As the class met for the first time, the participants introduced themselves and shared a bit of their story. When it was Claire's turn, she spoke fondly of the life she and Jug had shared together. She also mentioned how important her faith was to her. She then said, "I love Asbury. But I'm not sure I can join the church. You see, I've been a member of the same church since I was six weeks old. Changing churches is hard. Jug and I often talked about whether we should join or not. So I'm waiting for a sign—a sign from God to let me know what to do."

The following week, the class met again. I wasn't sure what Claire meant by God giving her a sign, but I wondered if it had happened. Claire shared again, "I'm just not sure if I will be joining the church next week. I'm still waiting for a sign."

The next Sunday was February 1, 2015—the day the new members were to join the church. I still had not heard anything from Claire about what she would be doing. So right before the worship service, I went into the sanctuary where she was seated. "Claire," I said, "I don't want you to feel pressured into joining the church. It's fine if you don't join. You'll always be a part of our church family. I just need to know if I should call your name with the New Member Class."

"Yes," she said with a smile, "I will be joining the church

today."

"Wonderful!" I said. As I walked back to put on my ministerial robe, I wondered if Claire had received her sign. Something, I suppose, had given her a sense of peace about the decision. And perhaps that's the sign she was looking for. Maybe she just needed a sense of peace about it all.

I noticed that Claire had been sitting beside a woman named Nancy, who also was joining the church that day. Claire actually had introduced Nancy to the church, and Nancy fell in love with Asbury. Her enthusiasm for the church bubbled over. Perhaps Claire saw what she had done for Nancy and realized she was at the right place at the right time. Perhaps this sense of ministry and purpose was an affirmation for Claire to join the church.

The service was about to start, and I quickly needed to go over the announcements with the person who would be presenting them. I reminded the announcer to be sure to mention that today we would be collecting money for the Souper Bowl of Caring Ministry. This special offering happens on the day of the Super Bowl, and the funds go to local food ministries for the homeless.

And then it dawned on me—today is the Super Bowl. Claire Knight will be joining the church on the day of the Super Bowl. If my old football coach wanted to give his wife some kind of a sign, I couldn't think of a better one!

I hustled back into the sanctuary to where Claire was sitting and said, "I don't know if you received a sign or not, but did you realize that today is the Super Bowl? How about that?" We both laughed.

It turns out that the sign Claire received during the week

was a sense of peace about it all. That's often how God influences and nudges us—through a gut feeling.

❦

But I believe we received another sign that Sunday. I can imagine Coach Jug Knight dancing up a storm as he celebrated his wife joining the church on the day of the Super Bowl!

Jug, we can't wait to join you on the dance floor again. Don't forget to bring the eggnog!

THE PHONE CALL

If there was a Mount Rushmore for Asbury Memorial Church, there is no doubt in my mind whose four faces would be on the side of Mount Asbury. It would be Nell Hagins, Harold Wiley, Virginia Holiday, and Elizabeth Lariscy—four long-time members who were key contributors to the church's transformation. These four persons experienced Asbury in its glory years in the 20th century, its twenty-five-year decline, its resurgence at the end of the century, and its vitality in the 21st century.

Nell Hagins ran the kitchen and about everything else at Asbury. This dedicated Christian worked tirelessly at the church. Sometimes it seemed as though Nell lived there. She loved her Lord, loved serving people, and loved Asbury Memorial. Nell passed away in 2014 at the age of 90.

Harold Wiley brought great warmth to our church. He greeted, hugged, and welcomed everyone. He also was a great mediator when there were disagreements between church members. He spent a lot of time visiting members in the hospital and in nursing homes. Everyone loved Harold, and he loved them. He made his transition in 2011 at the age of 88.

Virginia Holliday is still with us at the age of 92. She is our energizer bunny! She's constantly working at the church—sings in the choir, plays in the handbell choir—even does liturgical dance! She is Asbury's designated walker for the Wesley Community Centers' Love Walk to raise funds for this important ministry that helps low-income families. She is in charge of fixing the drinks for all of our church events, decorates the tables for our special meals, helps with church mailings and bulletins, and a thousand other things. She amazes everyone at the church.

Elizabeth Lariscy was the "lady" of the bunch. She gave our church a little class. Always dressing immaculately—she'd always top off her classy outfit with a bow in her hair. "Miss Elizabeth" was tall and regal. She really wasn't that tall, but seemed tall by the way she carried herself. She spoke with an elegant southern accent. She was in charge of our Altar Guild, which was the perfect fit for her. You always knew that the church altar would be looking beautiful and proper.

Elizabeth helped start the Busy Bees—a group of women who made clown dolls as a way to have fun and to raise funds for the church. Although the original purpose of the Busy Bees was to have fellowship, the selling of the clown dolls helped pay the church's bills during its lean years.

Elizabeth had long been a widow, who lived by herself. In 2008, at the age of 94, Elizabeth stopped driving, moved from her house, and went into an assisted living facility in Savannah named Marsh View. She soon became a big part of the Marsh View community. She was especially known for making beautiful beaded necklaces.

Elizabeth, who never used to miss a Sunday at church, had to stop attending our services. Church members, however, kept in touch. Two Asburians, John Naylor and David Grice, made it a weekly ritual to go see Elizabeth. Other members would periodically visit and bring flowers. Every December the congregation would go to Marsh View and sing Christmas carols to Elizabeth and all of the residents.

In 2014, Elizabeth celebrated her 100th birthday. As wonderful as it was for Elizabeth to see her second century of living, we all knew that she was becoming more and more frustrated. She had outlived most of her close friends. Due to her health, she was confined to a wheelchair. She could no longer do the things she wanted to do. Every time I would visit her she would say, "Billy, why am I still here? Why doesn't the Lord want me? Why doesn't the Lord take me? I'm ready."

This lament would become a ritual. I never knew quite how to respond other than to say that we loved her and that she was an inspiration to her family and to her church family. We'd talk about her children and grandchildren. We'd eventually start talking about what was happening at the church—letting her enjoy the latest news. And I would remind her that she had a lot to do with the renewal of Asbury. In fact, I will never forget the first Church Council meeting I attended there. Elizabeth was the one who said, "Billy, do whatever you want to do to bring us back," words a minister rarely gets to hear. After we did some new and radical things, I sometimes would tease Elizabeth and say, "I bet you regret saying those words now!" We would both laugh.

Everyone at the church loved Elizabeth. It was difficult to see her wondering why she was still on this earth when all of her close friends were gone. It was difficult to see this Busy Bee frustrated that she could no longer do the things she yearned to do. She so badly missed her husband, family members, and friends who had passed on many years before her.

❦

On June 17th, 2015, an aide at Marsh View named Tamakie was with Elizabeth in her apartment. Tamakie said she saw Elizabeth suddenly pick up the telephone and say, "Hello…Hello." Tamakie was puzzled because she did not hear the phone ring. But Elizabeth had picked it up anyway and said, "Hello." Then, after a moment, Elizabeth slowly hung up the phone.

Tamakie asked, "Who was it? Who was on the phone?"

Elizabeth looked at her and said, "It was God calling me home."

A few hours later, I went to see Elizabeth. I knocked on her door, but there was no answer. Elizabeth wasn't able to come to the door, but she would often sit in a chair in the front room. When you knocked on the door, you could hear Elizabeth say, "Come in." But on this day, there was no answer.

I decided to open the door to see if Elizabeth was asleep in her chair. The chair was empty. I continued to call her name as I walked into the small apartment and towards the bedroom. The bedroom door was open, and there was

Elizabeth in bed. She was not breathing. She had made her transition.

❦

That day, Elizabeth did not say to me, "Why am I still here? Why doesn't the Lord want me?"

Earlier that day, Someone or Something had let Elizabeth know that she was loved and that she was wanted.

Come home, come home;
you who are weary, come home;
earnestly, tenderly, Jesus is calling,
calling, O sinner, come home!

THE TEACHER WITH THE BEAUTIFUL EYES

This story probably should be classified as irony instead of synchronicity, but I really wanted to include it in this book. So forgive me for my expanded definition of synchronicity for this story. Though it may be lacking in synchronicity, it is a story that is packed with wonder and grace.

❦

Beth McIntosh is the executive director of the Savannah Speech and Hearing Center. The Center helps people in the Savannah community who have speech, language, and hearing problems. The Center opened in 1954, so it's been serving people in South Georgia for a long time. Beth contacted me and asked if I would serve on the board. I was glad to serve because what Beth didn't know—and what most people do not know—is that I am a Savannah Speech and Hearing alumnus.

As a youngster, I had great difficulty speaking. I actually didn't have a problem speaking; I just couldn't be understood. Consonants were my downfall. So in 1963, when I was four years old, my mother started taking me to the Center. It's still in the same little red brick building at the same location on East 66th Street.

The Teacher with the Beautiful Eyes

I had not been to the Savannah Speech and Hearing Center in almost 50 years. When I went to my first board meeting, it was like stepping back in time. You know how places can have their own distinctive aromas. Well, the Savannah Speech and Hearing Center smelled exactly the same as it did 50 years ago. The aroma ignited a flood of memories.

I remembered how the Center was divided into tiny rooms, just big enough for a teacher to work one-on-one with a student. I can't remember the name of my teacher, but I remember her smile, her red hair, and her beautiful eyes. Immaculately dressed, she looked and acted as though the time spent with me was the most important thing in the world to her.

Articulating words was very difficult for me. My pretty-eyed teacher knew how to stretch and push me while being gentle and compassionate at the same time. We would do lots of exercises together. She would walk over to a record player and place the needle on the album so I could listen to how words should be pronounced. She would point to various pictures on sheets of paper and have me try to pronounce the names of the objects. I specifically remember her pointing to a picture of a masked man who was carrying a bag of money. I tried to say the word, "robber" which came out "wahver." After she tried to help me say robber, she said, "But there's another name for a robber. What I really want you to say is the word 'thief'." Oh my, I really was in trouble with that one!

Part of the irony of this story is that my two chosen professions (acting and preaching) rely heavily on speech and being understood. I still have moments when I struggle with words. When I was an actor, I worked with a script. This allowed me to practice words that I struggled saying. Auditions were not so easy, because I was seeing a script for the first time. But once I was cast in a show, I had time to work on my "problem words" in the script.

I have a similar advantage as a minister. I write out my sermons in advance, so I know what words I will be using. There may be a word I need to use that is difficult for me to say, so I have the advantage of practicing it before I preach. And if there is a word that is challenging for me to pronounce, I may replace it with a word that is easier for me. For instance, the word "regularly" can sometimes be difficult for me to say, so I might replace it with the word "often." Sometimes I plan to say a word like "regularly" in the sermon, but if I feel tired or not focused when it is time to say it, I can replace the word in mid-sentence with a word that is easier for me to say.

Doing interviews and speaking without a script make me uncomfortable because I don't have the opportunity to practice pronouncing the words I may want to use. If I have to focus on the pronunciations of the words, I can easily lose my train of thought and not say what I want to communicate. So I am more comfortable speaking when I have a script or manuscript.

❦

After several classes with my pretty speech teacher, I had a jaw dropping experience. One day, as my mother and I were walking out of the Savannah Speech and Hearing Center to our car, my mother asked me how the class went. I told her that it went well, and that I really liked my teacher.

"She has the most beautiful eyes," I said. "But there's something different about her. Sometimes she kind of looks at me funny. It's strange."

My mother said, "Billy, you do know that your teacher is blind, don't you?"

Blind? How could she be blind? She put the record on the record player and played it. She pointed at the pictures for me to pronounce. She looked right at me. She couldn't be blind.

Do you remember the closing scene of the movie, *The Usual Suspects*? Throughout the film, Special Agent Kuzan has been interrogating Verbal in a messy office at the police station. Near the end of the movie, Kuzan releases Verbal, who leaves the police precinct. But then Agent Kuzan starts replaying the interview in his mind and realizes that the responses that Verbal gave to his questions were fabricated and inspired by items that were in the little office. He then realizes that Verbal is actually the mysterious Keyser Söze.

Well, after my mother stunned me with this incredible news about my teacher, I started mentally replaying the experiences I had with her in our little room. Now that I thought about it, her blindness explained some of her actions—like putting her left hand on the record before she put the needle down on it with her right hand. It explained why she would sometimes place her hand on the wall of our cubicle. Yet, had my mother not told me, I never would have known that my teacher was blind.

I cannot remember my teacher's name, and there doesn't

seem to be a record of her at the Center. I wish I could thank her. I wish I could let her know that the little boy she helped has performed in professional theatrical productions in New York City, has preached at Marble Collegiate Church, one of the oldest churches in the United States, and has sung the National Anthem at Madison Square Garden. I wish she knew that he is still practicing his words every single week as he prepares his sermons.

Here was a teacher with a disability helping a little boy with his disability. I will never forget the teacher with the beautiful eyes—who they said was blind, but who could see the potential in me.

THE CIRCLE OF LIFE AND BUTTERFLIES

One of the persons who greatly impacted the revitalization of Asbury Memorial UMC was a remarkable woman named Janice Gantt. Janice Arlene Gantt was an incredible force of nature. She started attending the church not long after I arrived in 1993 and immediately brought a positive attitude and hopeful spirit that was so needed.

Janice matched her attitude with action. She became the church lay leader, which is a position that wears many hats. Janice wore those hats proudly and even added a few more. She led all kinds of meetings, participated in the funerals of our members, helped with our children's programs, and was active in many other ways. She was a "people person" who knew how to make others feel comfortable, welcomed, and included. She was an incredible vessel of love, joy, and sunshine.

Janice also was skilled at encouraging people to be in ministry. She often told our church members to find their niche and passion. Her words and enthusiasm helped many other people at the church to get involved. And, of course, she led by example. Having her at the church was basically like having an associate minister on staff.

Somehow, Janice also found time to be very involved in

the community. She was active in many cultural and charitable organizations. She was a member of everything from the Savannah Board of Realtors to being a co-founder of the Savannah Bridge Run.

Janice also was known as the "Birthday Card Lady." Whenever a member of the church had a birthday, they would receive a card from Janice in the mail. She must have spent a fortune for cards and postage. You soon learned to open your card over a container because every card was filled with tiny, colorful stars and glitter—Janice's trademark.

She also was known as the "Butterfly Lady." Janice loved butterflies! She had butterflies everywhere. When you went to her house you felt like you were going to a "Butterfly Festival"—butterfly plaques and paintings decorated yard and house.

❦

Unfortunately, Janice was also a cancer patient. She had battled and overcome the disease several times, but in 2005 the disease was overwhelming. She continued to fight the disease with her sense of humor and her positive faith. She even had little butterflies painted all over her bald head after she lost her hair from chemotherapy.

As Janice's illness progressively worsened, she asked me to go to the funeral home to help her make her funeral arrangements. I was honored to do so.

Janice wanted every person who attended her funeral to have the opportunity to take some of her ashes. That way, the person could put the ashes at a place that was special for the two of them. I will never forget the look on the funeral director's face when Janice told him that she wanted her ashes to be divided up and put into 250 small vials! And, oh yes, each vial not only should contain her ashes; they also should contain glitter!

At first, the gentleman was in shock. As he continued to converse with Janice and continued to get to know her, he said, "Yes, we can do it. This would be very appropriate for you."

❦

Around 6:00 a.m. on Sunday, April 24, 2005, the ringing of our telephone woke me up. The voice on the other end of the phone said that Janice would be passing soon. I rushed to her house and was able to be with Janice as she took her last breath.

It was a difficult time for me. I had just lost a dear friend and my right arm in ministry. Janice Gantt had been one of the main reasons Asbury Memorial was able to turn the corner and grow again. I wondered how I was going to preach and lead a worship service later that morning. I was exhausted and emotionally spent.

As I left Janice's house and got into the car, I remembered the time that I got a boost from the radio when my cousin Butch died 12 years earlier. I sarcastically thought to myself, "Lord, I know this is silly. I'm not into testing you. But I am so down and so hurt that if there is a way you could give some inspiration through the radio, I would greatly appreciate it."

I turned on the radio not expecting to hear anything that would be appropriate for the moment. But to my surprise a song was on that was all about heaven. I had never heard it before—the station was not a religious station—yet here was an upbeat song about going to a better place—heaven.

After the "Radio Angels" had helped me again, I went home and crashed. I couldn't sleep long—I had a worship service to lead that morning. I was so tired that I didn't even make it to the bedroom. I opened the door to our house and fell asleep on the sofa in our den. I was fortunate that I didn't sleep through the entire worship service. Somehow, I woke up in time to put the finishing touches on my sermon and get to the church. I really believe it was "Angel Janice" who helped wake me up in time.

The sermon that Sunday was about the "priesthood of all believers." The main message was that every person should see themselves as a minister—that each one of us has gifts to share to help others and to further the kingdom of God on earth. As I was preaching, I realized that Janice was the epitome of what the sermon was about. I thought how ironic it was that Janice would make her transition on the morning that I preached on the "priesthood of all believers."

I concluded the sermon by saying, "No one believed in the 'priesthood of all believers' more than Janice Gantt. No one wanted more for each of you to find your niche—your calling—and then 'Go for it!'"

Those were three of Janice's favorite words, "Go for it!"

When she was young, Janice wanted to "go for it." She wanted to be an ordained minister. Unfortunately, at that time women were not encouraged to go into the ordained ministry. Periodically, I would encourage Janice to go back to school—to go to seminary and become a minister. I'd say, "It's not too late to go to seminary. You might as well get paid for all this work you're doing."

But she'd say, "No, it's important for me not to get paid for it. It's important for me not to be clergy—not to be paid staff."

I believe Janice wanted people to understand that you don't have to be an ordained minister to be in ministry. You can be a real estate agent who loves God—or a plumber or a mechanic. Just find your niche and go for it.

At 6:00 p.m. on Thursday, April 28, we held an incredible memorial service at Asbury in honor of the great lay leader. This was the service that Janice and I had planned several months before her death.

Right before we started the service, I got word that one of our church members, Trina Dodd, had just given birth to a baby girl named Jameson. I thought that it was a bit ironic and hopeful that, on the day of Janice's funeral, we also were celebrating a birth. Janice would have liked this living out of the circle of life.

After the memorial service was over, we had a reception in the social hall. Some of the members and I were talking about the coincidence of Janice's memorial service and the birth of a new Asbury child on the same day—the birth of Trina's daughter, Jameson.

Then, I remembered another interesting coincidence. Trina, the mother who gave birth, is an incredible dancer. Several years before, Trina had danced in our worship service to the song, "Circle of Life," from *The Lion King*. It was an amazing dance. And at the very end of the song—on the very last beat of the music—Trina held up a real live baby—her first born child, Skyler.

Late that night, after the reception, I went to the hospital to check on Trina and to meet her new-born child. After I had a chance to see baby Jameson, Trina asked me about Janice's memorial service.

This prompted me to say, "Isn't it neat that you gave birth on the day of Janice's memorial service and that you did that wonderful dance at the church to the song, 'Circle of Life?' And remember how you held your baby daughter, Skyler, up in the air at the end of the song?"

Trina looked at me and said, "Billy, that wasn't Skyler. We didn't use Skyler for that dance. That was Janice's grandson. The dance was about celebrating the life of Janice's grandson."

Trina and I looked at each other in awe and wonder. What I thought was a little wow moment suddenly turned into a bigger wow moment.

A close friend of Janice's later reminded me that the last funeral service that Janice participated in as lay leader was that of Trina's father, Robert Dodd. I later learned that Janice and Robert were friends at the same high school.

A beautiful bench made of granite was given to the church in honor of Janice. It sits in our courtyard for all to see. Engraved in it are Janice's name and a tiara—Janice liked to wear a glittery tiara on her birthday. Also, a really large butterfly is engraved on the back of the bench and two smaller ones are engraved on the seat. Words by Barbara Haines Howett are etched into the bench—words that formed one of Janice's favorite quotes—one she especially used near the end of her life: "Just when the caterpillar thought the world was over, she became a butterfly."

I will never forget the day the granite bench was delivered to the church and placed in the courtyard. A number of us were standing at the door looking at it when, all of a sudden, the biggest butterfly we'd ever seen flew down and landed on Janice's bench. We were amazed as it seemed to sit there for eternity.

Thanks be to God for butterflies, for the circle of life, and for Janice Gantt!

Rebecca and the Scarves

When Cheri and I first moved back to Savannah in 1991, I worked as an associate minister at Wesley Monumental United Methodist Church. Established in 1868, Wesley Monumental is a large, beautiful church on Calhoun Square in the heart of historic Savannah.

One October day in 1991, a church member named Nichola Coe approached me about a family that was going through a difficult time. Nichola was from England, and her husband, Dan, was the assistant director of the Savannah International Airport. They knew about a family that had flown from England to Savannah in an effort to save the life of their four-year-old daughter, Rebecca.

Nichola went on to tell me that Rebecca had brain cancer. The family flew to Savannah so she could have special medical care at Memorial Hospital. Nichola asked me if I would visit them. She said, "The parents are not 'church people' so I thought it would be good for a minister to go who wasn't very ministerial." I chuckled and told her that I understood and would be glad to see them.

I had no idea how the acceptance of this invitation would impact my life.

❦

Rebecca and the Scarves

As I stepped into Rebecca's hospital room, I saw a tiny girl sitting up in bed with many tubes attached to her. It was obvious that she had been through great trauma. Her head was completely shaved, and her face was very swollen—her left eye was almost swollen completely shut.

Then I heard a voice with a heavy English accent say, "Why did the hedgehog cross the road?"

I hadn't even had time to say "hello" or to introduce myself. I wasn't sure if the child in this cancer-attacked body was talking to me or to someone else. I just put one foot inside the door, and out came, "Why did the hedgehog cross the road?" I wasn't even sure what a hedgehog was.

"I'm sorry. What did you say?" I asked.

From her bed, the child said again, "Why did the hedgehog cross the road?"

Finally overcoming the shock that a child who was in horrible physical condition was telling me a joke, I said, "I don't know. Why did the hedgehog cross the road?"

"To get to the other side, silly!"

Then out came a laugh that sounded much older than a four-year-old's.

After having this surprise introduction to Rebecca, I saw two adults standing in the room. Then I noticed another child—a toddler—crawling on the floor. I introduced myself to the adults and learned that they were Rebecca's parents. They had been quietly observing the comedy act that Rebecca had given me. It was like, "This is our daughter. Isn't she amazing?" Then I learned that the caterpillar on the floor was Rebecca's younger brother.

Rebecca's parents had been taking care of their sick child

for a long time. Tumors had invaded her body. Treatments and surgeries had not gone well. I learned that they had read an article by a neurosurgeon in Savannah about a treatment that was not accessible in England. They flew to Savannah as a last effort to save their daughter's life.

Rebecca's parents were remarkable people in their own right. The love for their children was obvious. I felt very drawn to this family and their predicament. I thought about my daughter, Chelsea. I couldn't imagine what it would be like if she was in Rebecca's situation and if we had to fly to another country for help—not knowing a soul.

Remembering Nichola's words about the family being a bit skeptical of "religious people," I was concerned that they would be hesitant of receiving help. But as I continued to visit them and as we got to know each other, we were able to talk about some of their needs.

When Rebecca was well enough from her current medical crisis, she would continue chemotherapy treatments as an outpatient. She and her family would need a place to live. Once word of this need got out into the community, a generous Savannahian stepped up to the plate and donated her beach house on Tybee Island. The beach setting would give Rebecca and her family a therapeutic environment as they went through this difficult time together.

Since Rebecca would be receiving all kinds of medical care, the family would also have financial needs. With the help of members from Wesley Monumental, we established a trust fund for Rebecca at a bank. Then we contacted the local newspaper to do an article about her so that people were aware of her situation and could make donations.

My main job was to be a friend to the family and to try to make life as normal for them as possible in this horribly abnormal situation. So I introduced them to local things like our fresh seafood and Krispy Kreme Doughnuts. Of course, they quickly saw through my smokescreen and realized that I was getting them Krispy Kremes so I could eat them too.

We had a lot of laughs and good times together. But, of course, the time was also filled with tension because of Rebecca's condition. There were occasions when she would have to be rushed to the Emergency Room from Tybee. I remember one time in particular when it looked as though we might lose her. This was terribly difficult for all of us who grew close to this family. We couldn't imagine how difficult it was for her parents.

It became clear that Rebecca's treatments were not going well. We began to hope that she could at least live long enough to make it to Christmas and to her 5th birthday. Rebecca, you see, was a Christmas baby—born on Christmas Eve.

The Christmas season meant so much to Rebecca. She taught me all about Father Christmas, the English name for the personification of Christmas. She also introduced me to one of her favorite stories, *The Snowman*, by Raymond Briggs. *The Snowman* is a children's picture book without words that reveals the story of a young boy and his magical experience with a snowman. In 1982, it was adapted into a beautiful animated film. The story is told through pictures, action, and music. It is wordless like the book, except for a hauntingly beautiful song called, "Walking in the Air."

Rebecca made it to Christmas and to her 5th birthday, but on February 3, 1992, she made her transition. The loss was hard for many of us in the Savannah community. A memorial service was held at Wesley Monumental. The sanctuary was packed. This English child had touched so many lives.

Then Rebecca's parents said, "Billy, will you come to England to lead a memorial service there?"

I was touched by their invitation. Cheri and I flew to England for the service. Somehow Rebecca's parents found the strength not only to grieve and have a memorial service, but to host us and to make sure we got to experience many wonderful things in England.

We got to visit the house where John Wesley lived and died and got to see the tomb where he was buried. We toured Windsor Castle, and we saw two theatrical productions. We stayed at a bed and breakfast and had tea and scones. It was an experience we will always cherish. Cheri and I were so blessed by meeting Rebecca and her family.

The story of *The Snowman* that Rebecca loved ends very differently than our version of *Frosty the Snowman*. Frosty melts near the end of the story, but then later comes back to life because of another burst of winter magic. One could consider Frosty's resurrection a Christian metaphor for life after death.

In the English story of *The Snowman*, the story ends with the boy going outside to find his snowman friend melted—only a hat and scarf remain on a tiny mound of snow. In this poignant version, the snowman does not come back to life.

The boy has to wrestle with the sadness and pain of losing a loved one. But just before the credits roll at the end of the film, the little boy pulls a scarf out of the pocket of his bathrobe. The scarf had been given to him by Father Christmas when the Snowman took the boy on a great adventure. The boy holds the scarf and looks at it, remembering the blessings he had been given through the experiences he had with his icy friend.

A year after Rebecca's death, I became the pastor of Asbury Memorial. During my ministry at Asbury, I started pulling out scarf after scarf—things that reminded me of the blessings I had received from and through this unique child.

For instance, when we had very few members at the old inner city church, we were blessed to have a new couple named Ned and Helen Downing start attending our services. Ned was "Dr. Downing," a highly-thought-of neurosurgeon in Savannah, known for his great surgical skills. I learned that he was the surgeon who wrote the article that motivated Rebecca's family to come to Savannah. I also learned that he had trained in New York City where he and Helen were members of Marble Collegiate Church—long before I started working there. The Downings became key players in the revival of Asbury Memorial.

I found another beautiful scarf when a wonderful person named Anita Clay started attending the church. After she joined and became a member, I discovered that Anita was the person who donated her Tybee Beach house to Rebecca and her family when they needed a place to stay.

Another scarf appeared when Pam Parker Kress crossed

the ocean and came to Asbury. Pam moved to the United States from England and became another one of our key members. She leads a study group, sings in the choir, and visits people who are homebound or in nursing homes and hospitals. Pam happens to be the mother of Nichola Coe, the woman who first told me about Rebecca and her family and asked me to visit them.

You see, I keep pulling out scarf after scarf after scarf—it never seems to stop.

Some of the most important scarves that I pull out are things that were taught to me by a five-year-old "old soul"—things like: "Have Courage." "Laugh!" "Have fun every day!" "Do not take things for granted! Every day is a gift!" The Snowchild had taught us well!

On August 12, 1993, the year after Rebecca's death, another scarf appeared. Cheri gave birth to our second daughter, Christina *Rebecca* Hester.

The English child who battled cancer and who welcomed me with a joke continues to touch people's lives. I look forward to being with her again one day—walking in the air.

Childhood Wows

There are probably many wow moments that happened in my life long before I started taking them seriously in my twenties. No telling how many experiences of grace, wonder, and synchronicity I had as a child. Unfortunately, most of these experiences have disappeared from my memory. Two incidents, however, will always remain with me because of the strong emotions attached to them.

When I was nine years old, my mother enrolled me in the Big Brothers program at our local YMCA. Since my father had died when I was four, my mother was concerned about me not having enough experiences with male role models. I, of course, had experiences with my male relatives and with the men at our church. But it had been five years since my father's death, and she wanted me to have more opportunities with male mentors.

The "Big Brother" I was given was a man who was married and had a family. He was also the leader of a Boy Scout Troop. As a scoutmaster, he obviously was fond of outdoor activities. So on one of our first outings, he took me camping. He picked me up at my house on 65th Street, and we drove to a campground on either St. Simon's or Jekyll Island. Both coastal islands are next to each other and are about an hour and a half south of Savannah.

After getting out our gear and setting up the large tent, we cooked supper and played cards. We had a good time—the man seemed nice. When it was time for bed, I took my sleeping bag into the tent and went on the opposite side from where he was.

"Oh, you don't need to go way over there," he said. "Why don't you put your sleeping bag here?" He gestured to a space not far from him.

I didn't think much about it, but you can probably see where this is going. During the middle of the night, before I had fallen into a deep sleep, the man started molesting me. I wasn't sure what to do. I pretended to be asleep.

A thousand thoughts ran through my head: What can I do? What should I do? Should I pretend to stay asleep? Should I open my eyes and tell him to stop? But what if he is mad—what if he hurts me? What if he threatens to kill me or my family if I tell anyone?

Or should I run out of the tent and try to talk to someone? But what if they don't believe me? No one knows me here. I am far from home. And this man would have me to himself and could hurt me. What should I do?

Not knowing what to do, I kept my eyes closed and silently prayed. I hoped that he would not try to wake me up. If he knew that I knew what he was doing, I wasn't sure how he would react.

After what seemed to be an eternity, the man stopped touching me. He rolled away from me and fell asleep. The only problem now was that we were to stay there another night. How was I going to get through it?

The questions continued to flow through my nine-year-old mind. Can I last through this one more night? What if he wants me to be awake while he's touching me, and he tries to wake me up? What will happen if he knows that I know what he is doing to me? Should I try to sneak off during the day and tell someone? Should I pretend to be sick and need to go home? But he may become suspicious and realize that I know what he did. What to do?

What happened next is as clear to me as though it happened yesterday. After we cooked and ate breakfast the next morning, an old man came up to my "Big Brother" and started talking to him. They were in conversation for a good 10 to 15 minutes. Then my "Big Brother" came over to me and said, "Billy, I'm sorry. I made a mistake. I didn't make a reservation for tonight, and they are all filled up. I didn't realize that so many people would be camping. I'm afraid we're going to have to pack up and go back to Savannah."

Using my best acting skills, I tried to look disappointed. "That's too bad," I said. "But don't worry. We can come back another time."

Well, of course, there was no other time. As soon as I got home, my mother could tell that something was wrong. It took her a while to get it out of me, but I finally told her what had happened. Needless to say, that was the last I ever heard about the Big Brothers program.

I have often wondered what would have happened had the man and I stayed another night. Could I have gotten through it again? Would I have tried to fight him? Would I have gotten hurt?

One of the greatest gifts I have ever received was an old man who came bearing what he thought was bad news. The bad news, of course, was good news. What he thought was bad timing was *perfect* timing. I wish there was some way I could have let him know how God used him that day. He may have saved my life.

Before I move on to the second childhood story that involves grace, wonder, and synchronicity, I want to be clear in saying that I believe that Big Brothers is a good organization. There are many more positive experiences from it than negative ones. The program I was part of was brand new and had growing pains. Plus, back in the 1960s, people didn't talk about child molestation as much as we do now. People didn't know much about the psychiatric disorder of pedophilia. Just be sure that if you are ever involved with such programs that they have a good screening and evaluation process.

I have heard many people mistakenly link pedophilia with homosexuality. This was one of the arguments used to justify the Boy Scouts of America's policy to exclude gay scouts and scoutmasters—which is a bit ironic since I was molested by a *straight scoutmaster*.

It's important for people to be aware that statistics show that most pedophiles are heterosexual. Some studies have it as high as 90% or higher. Part of this overwhelming percentage, of course, has to do with there being a lot more straight people in the world than gay people. But it is important to debunk the myth about gays and pedophiles that has been spread for decades. Pedophilia is not related to one's sexual orientation.

The other childhood wow moment that has stayed in my memory throughout the years occurred about a year after the previous story—when I was about ten years old.

As a child, I had a huge crush on a girl named Beth. Beth and I grew up at the same church. We dated from age 5 to age 12. Yes, you read it right—from age 5 to 12. I know it's strange. We were odd children. But this was serious! We would actually go out on dates. Since neither of us could drive, our parents would drop us off at the movies or Putt-Putt or dinner at Shoney's. I can't tell you how many birthday gifts, Christmas presents, and valentine cards I bought Beth over the years.

When I was ten years old, I learned that Beth was going to a religious summer camp for a week at the Effingham County campground. When I found out this news, I said, "Mom, sign me up!" Visions of being with Beth for seven straight days danced in my head!

Then I said to mom, "What is Effingham County?"

Today, Effingham County feels like a suburb of Savannah. But back in the 1960s, Effingham County was a "fer piece away"—especially for a ten-year-old. It was only 27 miles from Savannah, but to me, it seemed halfway across the country.

The Effingham County United Methodist Campground is one of the oldest religious campgrounds in the country. The original campground was built in 1790; but, in 1864, Sherman and his troops burned it on their "March to the Sea." The campground was at two other locations until it was relocated to 18 acres of land in Springfield, Georgia, in 1907. It has a large, open-air tabernacle with overhead fans and wooden pews. "Tents" or cabins line the perimeter of the grounds.

The particular camp I attended was during the middle of the summer, and it was hot—REAL hot. There were very few trees for shade, and the cabins we stayed in had no air conditioning. I did not know a soul at the camp other than Beth, and we were put into two separate groups. I hardly got to see her the whole time I was there. I was miserable and homesick—with an emphasis on the word "sick."

I always had a difficult time being away from home as a child. This was probably connected to the loss of my father at such a young age. To be far from home and to be so unhappy was not a good combination. I cried myself to sleep every night. I even cried at times during the day, trying to hide my tears from the adults and the other children at the camp. I felt ashamed and embarrassed that I couldn't be like all the other kids, who seemed to be having the time of their lives. What was wrong with me? Why did I cry so much? Why couldn't I be as happy and as strong as the other kids?

After struggling through the camp for about four days, I finally heard some good news. I learned that on Sunday, the Savannah district superintendent was coming to preach at Camp Meeting.

This was good news because I knew the Savannah district superintendent. His name was Rev. Ned Steele. Rev. Steele's family attended my home church in Savannah. I knew his three daughters. The older two were close friends of my sister, Wendy.

Rev. Steele was a handsome man known for his intellect and sense of humor. He was from the South but had attended Yale Divinity School. He was loved and respected by everyone. I couldn't wait to see him—at last, a familiar face! Sunday couldn't come soon enough!

I didn't get to see Rev. Steele before the worship service. He was probably tucked away in a cabin that had air conditioning as he thought about the message he would be bringing the people that Sunday. I saw him walk to the front of the big tabernacle as the service was about to start. It was good to see him, even from afar. It was especially good to see him standing behind the pulpit. It was good to hear him too. He had a strong voice with a rich resonance, while at the same time, it was soothing.

About halfway through the sermon, something strange started happening. Rev. Steele's voice started cracking. Rev. Steele started pausing. His face began to turn red. Then a boatload of tears started rolling down his cheeks. He paused again and again. The floodgates opened, and Rev. Steele took out a handkerchief and wiped away the tears. Something was terribly wrong. This certainly wasn't part of the sermon.

Through his tears, Rev. Steele began to explain what was happening. He apologized and said that he had been away from his family. He had been on the road traveling—attending event after event. He said that he hadn't been able to be with his family for a long time and that he was terribly homesick—that he greatly missed his wife, Evelyn, and their three daughters, Suzanne, Sally, and Sandra. I sat there dumbfounded. Rev. Steele was crying. Rev. Steele was homesick.

Rev. Steele may have felt bad about his tears. He was probably concerned that they got in the way of the message of the sermon. But it is the most memorable sermon I have ever heard—and the most impactful. Rev. Steele had been a "wounded healer." His tears and honest feelings lifted the spirit of a lonely, afraid, ten-year-old boy. I no longer was ashamed. I knew that I was okay and that I would be fine.

After the service, I went up to Rev. Steele and told him how much the sermon had meant to me. He chuckled. He probably thought I was crazy since his sermon was more like a "cryathon." But, of course, he did not know what I had experienced that week.

A couple of years later, Rev. Steele and his family would move to a new district. I wouldn't see him again for over fifteen years. But we stayed in touch, mostly through letters. He was a wonderful letter writer.

When I moved to New York, he was very interested in my acting career and the fact that I was attending Marble Collegiate Church. When I made my decision to go to Princeton Seminary, he was one of the first persons I called. He followed my progress through seminary and into my ordination and ministry.

I always felt his support. I always felt a special kinship with him. Most ministers in the South Georgia Conference attend a seminary in the South. Very few attend seminaries in the Northeast. Ned was a Georgia boy who had gone to Yale and then returned to his Southern roots. I was a Georgia boy who went to Princeton who also came back to South Georgia. Our paths had many similarities.

❦

In 2003, I got a phone call from Ned's daughter, Suzanne, letting me know that her father had died. He was 89. Suzanne said that there would be a funeral in Macon, Georgia, where Ned and Evelyn had been living. The burial, however, would be in Savannah, his hometown. "Oh, yes," I said. "I had forgotten that your dad was from Savannah.

Then Suzanne said, "We want to have another memorial service for dad in Savannah. We were wondering if we could have it at Asbury Memorial since that was Dad's home church."

"Asbury was your father's home church?" I asked.

"Yes, that's where he grew up. In fact, it was at the altar at Asbury where he accepted his call for the ministry as a young man."

❦

It's funny how things sometime end up. The Effingham County Campground has become one of my favorite places. In the early 1990's, I was asked to be the song leader for the week of Camp Meeting. I wound up being the song leader for about five years in a row. I came to love the history of the campground, the people of the campground, the food of the campground, and, of course, the great singing of the campground. There's nothing like Camp Meeting singing! And over the years, I've heard some mighty good sermons at the campground. But none have blessed me more than the sermon I heard when I was ten years old—a sermon from the man who answered his call to ministry at the altar of the church where I am now preaching—an altar where two homesick preachers have often knelt.

Epilogue: The Gospel According to You

As I mentioned in the introduction of this book, the psalmists in the Hebrew Scriptures did not hesitate to express their feelings to God. I believe this openness and honesty with God is important. Many of us grew up being taught that we shouldn't let God see us at our worst. But the psalmists received strength and healing, not by covering up their feelings, but by expressing them.

In seminary, I read a phrase that has always meant a lot to me: "The atheist may complain, but the believer can protest." The atheist has no one to express his or her hurt feelings to, but the believer does. So ultimately our expressions of anger and frustration are affirmations of faith. It's no wonder we feel better after expressing our feelings to God.

But the psalmists did something else to strengthen their faith: they remembered the things God had done for them. In fact, they used this technique even more than they used the laments.

Over and over again, the psalmists are thanking God for creating the world, for saving them from their enemies, for doing acts of justice, for giving them dominion over the earth—the list goes on and on. They are constantly thanking the Lord for all of God's wonderful deeds. It is remembering what God had done for them that offers them strength and faith for the present and future.

Each of us can benefit from remembering what God has done for us. I encourage you to create a WOW! Journal that helps you remember how you've been blessed. Just as we benefit from reading The Gospel According to Matthew, Mark, Luke, or John, you will benefit from reading "The Gospel According to You!" Just as the four Gospels include experiences of God and how God has impacted lives, you can do the same for your life. Your Gospel is just as important.

As I was working on the manuscript for this book, a friend emailed me a remarkable story. Ironically, he didn't know that the book I was working on was about wow moments. I'm not even sure he knew I was writing a book.

The story he sent was about Jennifer Bricker, a young woman who was born without legs. Jennifer's natural parents abandoned her on the day she was born. When she was three months old, she was adopted by Sharon and Gerald Bricker, two loving and supportive parents.

As Jennifer got older, she discovered she had a passion for gymnastics. One might think that gymnastics would be the last thing a child without legs should pursue, but not Jennifer and her parents. In fact, Jennifer would go on to excel in gymnastics, volleyball, basketball, and softball. She even won the Illinois State High School Tumbling Championship. That, in itself, is a wow story. But it gets better.

As a youngster, Jennifer's idol was Dominique Moceanu, the great Romanian-American gymnast. Jennifer was Dominique's biggest fan. She wanted to be just like her. During the 1996 Atlanta Olympics, Jennifer started to watch her idol avidly. When Jennifer's parents started watching the Olympics with her, they realized that the gymnast their daughter loved so much had the same last name that Jennifer had when they adopted her—Moceanu. It didn't take them long to realize that the great gymnast they were watching was actually Jennifer's sister.

So in December of 2003, Jennifer sent Dominique a large envelope that contained a typed letter, a bundle of photos, and some court documents. When Dominique first opened it, she thought she was being sued. But then she read the letter. Jennifer explained the situation and what had happened. She, of course, let Dominique know that she had a sister—that *she* was her sister.

Dominique read the letter over and over again. She couldn't believe it. Her first response was disbelief. Then she became angry at her parents for not telling her about her baby sister. Eventually, Dominique would contact Jennifer, and now the two sisters, who grew up a thousand miles from each other, have a close relationship.

Now that's a double-wow story!

Recently making national news was the story of Kelvin Lewis and Alfonso Slater. Both Kelvin and Alfonso grew up in Mozambique. Both boys were put in an orphanage in Africa because their parents died of AIDS. There, at the age of four, the young boys became best friends.

In 2008, Alfonso, at the age of 10, was adopted by parents from the United States. 10,000 miles now separated these close friends who had been there for each other through tragedy. Six months later, Kelvin, who was also 10, was adopted by a different family. You can imagine everyone's surprise when it was discovered that both boys were adopted by families from the same town—Gilbert, Arizona. They live within two miles of each other. The boys, now 18, go to the same high school, play on the same soccer team, and plan to be roommates when they attend Brigham Young University. It's quite a remarkable story.

Wow moments are happening all the time. And they are happening to you. Will you remember them? Will you allow them to strengthen your faith?

You've read some of my stories. Now, it's your turn. Create your own WOW! Journal. If you can remember any of your wow moments from the past, write them down. When you experience a wow moment in the future, write it down. Add it to your journal.

There may be occasions in your life when you will say, "My God, my God, why have you forsaken me?" But you will have a new tool to turn to for help—a resource that will remind you of God's love and faithfulness.

As I mentioned previously, we are blessed to have a number of resources to help us experience the presence of God. One of those resources is the Bible. But what is the Bible? It is a book filled with stories of grace—of miracles—of wow moments!

God is just as active in our lives today as God was in the

lives of Abraham, Sarah, Moses, Jesus, Peter, Martha, Mary, and Paul. As writer Paula D'Arcy puts it, "God comes to you disguised as your life."

So record how God is working in your life. Then, when you have moments of despair and sorrow, you have another life preserver to offer you strength and encouragement.

Go forth with your eyes and ears and hearts open! Be attentive to the wow moments in your life, and write them down. You will be blessed by "The Gospel According to You."

About the Author

Billy Hester has been senior minister of Asbury Memorial United Methodist Church in Savannah, Georgia, since 1993. He received a BFA in Theatre from Valdosta State College in 1981. After having a theatrical career in New York, he attended Princeton Theological Seminary where he received a Master of Divinity in 1989. He then served at Marble Collegiate Church, church of Dr. Norman Vincent Peale, in New York City before moving back to his hometown of Savannah, Georgia, where he has served at Wesley Monumental UMC, Wesley Oak UMC, and Asbury Memorial UMC. He and his wife, Cheri, have four adult children: Chelsea, Christi, Wendell, and Wesley—and five dogs: Simon, Pablo, Angel, Rusty, and Gingy.

Resources

Now that you've read Billy's first book, you may wish to explore his life and ministry further. This chapter provides several resources with more information about subjects he mentions in the book.

At www.asburymemorial.org, you can find information about Billy's Asbury Memorial ministry, with video segments from the worship services, including his inspiring sermons. Information about Asbury Memorial Theatre is also there.

Billy mentioned several songs in his stories. You may enjoy seeing YouTube videos of them. Suggestions follow:

- From the chapter, "The Song:"
  "You'll Never Walk Alone," Josh Groban on PBS
  —www.youtube.com/watch?v=oCTo04Yc1IY
- From the chapter, "The Pipe Organ:"
  "Hallelujah Chorus," Opera Company of Philadelphia and Macy's Wanamaker Grand Court Organ
  —www.youtube.com/watch?v=wp_RHnQ-jgU
- From the chapter, "The Circle of Life and Butterflies:"
  "Heaven," Los Lonely Boys

—www.youtube.com/watch?v=AFpaRyxHcO8

- From the chapter, "Rebecca and the Scarves:"
  "Walking in the Air," from *The Snowman*
  —www.youtube.com/watch?v=ubeVUnGQOIk

For a flashback to one of Billy's New York City experiences, here's a 1989 article from the *New York Times* about his upcoming first sermon at Marble Collegiate Church:
—tinyurl.com/jr5qhjq.